Involving Families in School Mathematics

Readings from "Teaching Children Mathematics,"
"Mathematics Teaching in the Middle School,"
and "Arithmetic Teacher"

Involving Families in School Mathematics

Readings from "Teaching Children Mathematics,"
"Mathematics Teaching in the Middle School,"
and "Arithmetic Teacher"

Edited by
Douglas Edge

Nanyang Technological University
National Institute of Education
Singapore 259756

NATIONAL COUNCIL OF TEACHERS OF MATHEMATICS
Reston, Virginia

Copyright © 2000 by
THE NATIONAL COUNCIL OF TEACHERS OF MATHEMATICS
1906 Association Drive, Reston, VA 20191-9988
www.nctm.org
All rights reserved

Library of Congress Cataloging-in-Publication Data:
ISBN: 0-87353-491-3

Printed in the United States of America

Table of Contents

Introduction

The National Council of Teachers of Mathematics (NCTM) for many years has published articles that address family involvement in the mathematics education of children. Sometimes the authors discuss and summarize the main reasons why families and teachers benefit from the shared learning experience. Other authors focus on specific strategies and activities that involve parents or caregivers who either come to their children's school or help their children in some special way at home.

Many teachers and other curriculum planners also have strongly endorsed the initiatives that facilitate family members' participation in their children's mathematics learning and have been very successful in developing and implementing exceptional programs that further the goals of family participation. The purpose of this book therefore is to present a collection of articles that highlight helpful strategies and ideas and that describe some of these successful programs. Ultimately it is hoped that others may be inspired by some of the success stories and will choose to embark on initiatives of their own.

Part 1: Families and School Mathematics

In the first section of this book, the articles present the reader with rationales for involving families in school mathematics and suggest ways in which this participation might be accomplished. For example, Peressini uses a framework of functional approaches that include communicating, volunteering, learning at home, and community collaboration. Bratina, as well as Goldstein and Campbell, acknowledging that students' academic success improves with family involvement, offers tips on how to increase one's effectiveness when helping children with homework. In one other article, De La Cruz outlines a research-based model that was used successfully to promote the participation of Latino families in the mathematics learning of their children.

Part 2: Family Participation in School Settings

Perhaps the most familiar school-based family-participation activity is Family Math Night. Two articles in this section, one by Reys and Wasman, and another by Koes and Saab, describe successful implementations of variations of these events: a mathematics fair and an olympics. School-based family participation, however, can take other forms—seminars or workshops, for example. Some seminars encourage children to attend along with their parents or caregivers; other workshops are intended for adults only. De La Cruz, in her article in the previous section, details one such example. Another approach adopted by some schools involves establishing a lending library of children's books that in some way involve mathematics themes. McCarty presents a rationale for her school's library project and gives a helpful list of specific books to sample.

Part 3: Family Participation in Home Settings

The articles in this third section relate to home settings and often pertain to specific mathematical topics such as problem solving, patterning, early number concepts, geometry, and measurement. Ashlock, however, suggests ways for families to attend to the mathematics topics using informal settings in and around the home. In another article, Orman describes the development of, and the responses to, mathematics backpacks that she prepared for home use by her students.

Part 4: Appendixes

The final few pages of this book contain three appendixes. The articles listed in the first appendix have all been selected from *Arithmetic Teacher* or *Teaching Children Mathematics*, and all complement or supplement in some way the articles chosen for publication in this collection. The second appendix lists articles published in the February 1998 focus issue of *Teaching Children Mathematics*. The focus issue contains articles, several reprinted in this collection, as well as references, activity ideas, and bibliographies all relating in some way to parent, community, and business and industry involvement in children's mathematics education. The third appendix lists other relevant books and includes references to Family Math books and to appropriate sections in several NCTM "Ideas" books.

Effective partnerships that develop among members of our mathematics education community, especially those between families and teachers, do result in significantly increased learning for our children. It is hoped that the readings and references collected in this book will be useful and will result in the creation of other wonderful mathematics learning experiences for everyone involved.

Part 1
Families and School Mathematics

What's All the Fuss about Involving Parents in Mathematics Education?

Dominic D. Peressini

Recent reform recommendations for education have become more inclusive as they call for parents, families, and the community at large to become involved in efforts to improve schools (e.g., National Parent-Teacher Association [1994]; U.S. Department of Education [U.S. DOE] [1994]). Indeed, the national education goals for the year 2000 suggest that educators foster partnerships among schools and parents:

Dominic Peressini, dominic.peressini @colorado.edu, teaches undergraduate and graduate classes in education at the University of Colorado, Boulder, CO 80309. He specializes in school mathematics reform, authentic assessment, learning to teach mathematics, and parent-community involvement in the process of education.

Every school will promote partnerships that will increase parental involvement and participation in promoting the social, emotional, and academic growth of children (U.S. DOE 1994, 2).

Accordingly, the school mathematics community has also begun to acknowledge the importance of including parents and the community in efforts to reform mathematics education (Burrill 1996; Price 1996). These calls for parental and community involvement, however, are often couched in vague terms that remain at an abstract level. Consequently, no clear role is identified for parents in their children's mathematics education. The purpose of this article is to delineate the possible roles of parents in school mathematics as we continue to implement the vision of reform-based mathematics education embodied in the NCTM's three *Standards*

documents (1989, 1991, 1995). In particular, I examine the rationale that undergirds efforts to involve parents in the process of education and the different types of parental involvement in mathematics education. I use the terms *parents* and *parental involvement* throughout this article. I recognize, however, that other adults may carry the primary responsibility for a child's health, development, and education. Therefore, all references to parents and parental involvement are meant to include all adults who play an important caretaker role in a child's home life.

Why Involve Parents in School Mathematics?

The attention being paid to increasing parental participation is grounded in a

5

number of positive consequences that are thought to coincide with family involvement in a child's education. Much of the interest regarding parents' involvement in their children's education centers on the argument that such involvement benefits students by increasing their academic achievement (Chavkin 1993; Henderson and Berla 1994). A significant body of research regarding parental involvement in education has been directed at the relationship between involvement and achievement. Many studies conclude that parental involvement is a key factor in a child's academic success. Others argue, however, that the positive relationship between parental involvement and student achievement has not been established quite yet (Madigan 1994). This argument is based on the notion that many studies examining the correlation between parental involvement and student achievement have neither carefully controlled for the different types of parental involvement that may take place nor used consistent definitions of student achievement—various studies have used grades, scores on standardized tests, homework completion, and a variety of other measures (Henderson and Berla 1994).

It is certain, however, that different forms of parental involvement do affect factors that may in turn affect student achievement or lead to a more enriched educational experience. A number of studies have suggested that parents' involvement in their children's education assists in improving levels of student health (Chavkin 1993), reducing student dropout rates (Rich 1985), fostering positive attitudes toward learning and school (Sattes 1985), increasing parent-child communication (Clark 1983; Scott-Jones 1984), promoting productive student behaviors (Comer and Haynes 1992; Swap 1993), enhancing the educational experiences of "disadvantaged" students (Liontos 1992; Moles 1993), and changing schools and curricula so that they better reflect

diverse student populations and are more multicultural (Comer 1980; Delgado-Gaitan 1990; Ogbu 1990; Filmore 1990).

In addition, some scholars argue that it is a basic right of all parents to be involved in the process of public education or, for that matter, in any decision that affects their lives (Sarason 1995). Related to this basic right of parents to be involved in their children's education is the notion that allowing parents to exercise this right—and in the process, to gain ownership over their children's educational experiences—increases home and community support for schools and their efforts to enhance their programs. The mathematics education community has recognized the importance of garnering this support and views parental involvement as necessary in increasing public support for the ongoing school-mathematics-reform agenda (Peressini 1996; in press). This perspective is apparent in a recent report of the NCTM's president (Price 1996, 606):

> What has been most distressing since we released the *Standards* documents is that our efforts to inform parents better have fallen short.... We have to help those parents bridge their fears and encourage them to join hands in providing a solid mathematics education for all children.

What Does Parental Involvement Look Like?

The term *parental involvement* has been used to refer to a variety of activities along a number of dimensions (Bloch and Tabachnick 1994; Epstein 1994; Lareau 1989). This wide use of the term has resulted in its becoming a "catchword that is relatively ill-defined," and it is quickly on its way to becoming another rhetorical notion in the reform of education (Bloch and Tabachnick 1994, 264). Epstein (1994), however, has devised a typology of the different forms of parental involvement. She classifies parental involvement into six func-

tional types: (1) parenting, (2) communicating, (3) volunteering, (4) learning at home, (5) community collaboration, and (6) decision making. The categories 2–6 serve as a framework that can guide mathematics educators in involving their students' parents in mathematics education. The first category, parenting, refers to the support that families provide for their children: ensuring their children's health and safety; developing parenting skills and child-rearing approaches that prepare children for school and that maintain healthy child development across grades; and building positive home conditions that support learning and behavior throughout the school years. Schools often help a variety of families with these parenting skills through workshops and outreach programs. However, this type of involvement is most often outside the classroom teacher's realm and is usually not a component of a mathematics teacher's parent-involvement strategies.

Communicating

Communicating involves the establishment of clear and open interaction between schools and homes. This type of involvement is perhaps the most common way in which teachers have traditionally involved parents in mathematics education. Maintaining open lines of communication between classrooms and families is essential as the changes outlined in the NCTM's *Standards* documents (1989, 1991, 1995)—which advocate a curriculum that is very different from what most parents experienced as learners of mathematics—are implemented. One effective avenue for mathematics teachers to communicate with their students' parents is through mathematics newsletters.

These newsletters can be created by individual teachers, groups of teachers by grade level, or the mathematics department. The newsletters can be published weekly, monthly, or quarterly. Newsletters often contain updates on what is occurring in mathematics

WHAT'S ALL THE FUSS ABOUT INVOLVING PARENTS IN MATHEMATICS EDUCATION?

7

classrooms, descriptions and explanations of curricular content and teaching methods, samples of students' work, student-written articles, sections for parents' questions, and invitations to parents to visit the mathematics classroom. A portion of a newsletter developed by Lehrer and Shumow as part of the Cognitively Guided Instruction (CGI) project is contained in figure 1.

Communication between the mathematics classroom and families can

Fig. 1. Parent newsletter

also be accomplished through a number of other strategies:

- Establishing networks of families that serve to keep one another informed regarding what is occurring in their children's mathematics classrooms. These networks give some parents, who may feel uncomfortable contacting teachers or who may not have the time, an alternative means of receiving information about their children's mathematics education.
- Organizing back-to-school nights when families can come to the school to hear about the mathematics program and instruction (see, e.g., Hall and Acri [1995, 8–10]).

These presentations may include teachers' teaching actual lessons and students' engaging in mathematics activities. Such programs allow parents to experience firsthand the changes in mathematics curriculum, instruction, and assessment.
- Offering formal and informal parent-teacher conferences in which individual students can be discussed and the mathematics programs can be examined in detail.
- Including written comments on an individual student's grade reports, which reflect on each student's mathematical development.
- Sending home mathematics portfolios of student work—or discussing them during parent-teacher conferences—which may include written work, projects, assessments, and other activities to help parents better understand what their children are encountering in the mathematics classroom.

It is essential, however, that communication not be limited to teachers' informing parents. Although informing parents is important, parents must be afforded an opportunity to respond to this communication and ask questions when necessary. Moreover, parents have an abundance of knowledge about their children's skills, interests, and backgrounds that when shared with the mathematics teacher can provide a more robust understanding of each individual student. This understanding can then be used as the teacher takes into account students' prior experiences when developing mathematics activities and individualizing instructional strategies. Hence, communication from home to school, as well as communication from school to home, is imperative in the successful involvement of families. Two-way communication ensures that parents are aware of what their children are experiencing in the mathematics

classroom, have various avenues to voice their concerns, and are able to contribute relevant information to their children's mathematics education.

Volunteering

Volunteering refers to parents' and families' volunteering, observing, or both, at the school or in other locations, to support students, teachers, programs, and the school. Encouraging parents to become active in the mathematics classroom is a powerful way of helping them understand the changes in their children's mathematics education. Volunteering not only garners support for the classroom teacher's efforts to implement reformed mathematics instruction, but parent volunteers also supply mathematics teachers with a valuable resource that can assist them in meeting the challenging demands of being a classroom teacher. In addition, by involving a variety of students' parents in the mathematics classroom, the school culture can more accurately reflect the diverse cultures of its student population.

Mathematics teachers can engage in a number of activities that focus on this type of parental involvement at the classroom and school level. Some of the many approaches include creating "parent rooms" at the school; emphasizing an open mathematics classroom in which parents feel comfortable to drop in and observe a mathematics lesson; and using parent volunteers in classrooms to help students with their mathematics assignments, create mathematics bulletin boards, and participate in the daily mathematics lesson. Parents can also facilitate lessons that incorporate their unique backgrounds and professional experiences, guide field trips to their working environments, and help develop integrated curriculum activities that reflect their personal or professional interests.

Learning at home

Learning at home involves parents' monitoring and assisting their children with learning activities at home, including homework and other curricular-linked activities and decisions. Assisting with their children's home assignments might be the most common way that parents expect to be involved in mathematics education. However, as mathematical content and pedagogy continue to develop and change, parents may find themselves on unfamiliar ground when they attempt to work with their children on mathematics.

Mathematics teachers can assist parents in their efforts in a number of ways. Organizing and offering activities that are meant to be completed by both the parent and the student can make parents' efforts to be involved at home more productive (see, e.g., Lazerick and Seidel [1996, 141]). This approach offers guidance for parents when they become involved in their children's mathematics assignments and allows parents and children to learn from each other as they progress through the activities.

Sometimes, when parents assist their children with their mathematics assignments, they unknowingly do it in a fashion that does not support what the mathematics teacher is trying to accomplish in the classroom. For example, rather than let children struggle with the mathematics needed to solve a problem and come up with their own solution, parents may show their children a procedure for solving the problem or simply give the answer. Mathematics teachers can overcome this tendency by offering suggestions and techniques for parents to use when they help their children with mathematics assignments. This guidance is often accomplished at back-to-school nights or when parents come to the school and observe the classroom teacher helping students.

Another example of home involvement is the *Family Math* program (Stenmark, Thompson, and Cossey 1986). This well-organized program focuses on parents' and children's learning mathematics together. In addition, it allows parents to experience and begin to understand the type of reformed mathematics that their children are learning. A typical *Family Math* experience includes six to eight sessions, led by a classroom teacher or experienced volunteer, in which parents and their children develop problem-solving skills and mathematical understanding in different contexts. *Family Math* books are also available for home use. These books contain an assortment of mathematics activities that assist parents' and children's home learning. An example of a *Family Math* activity, focusing on estimation and metric measurement, is presented in figure 2.

These types of home activities, in which parents not only monitor but also participate in the completion of mathematics activities, are essential in keeping parents informed about their children's mathematics education and affording them an opportunity to experience the power of mathematics in collaboration with their children.

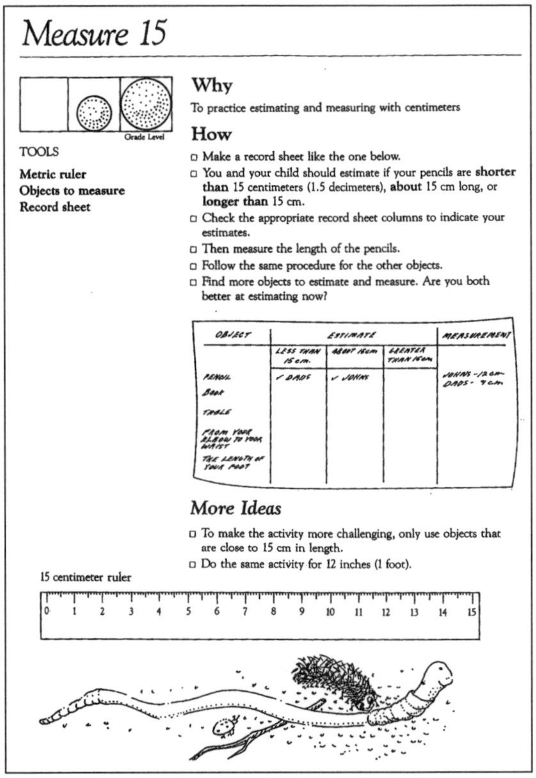

Measure 15

Grade Level

TOOLS

Metric ruler
Objects to measure
Record sheet

Why

To practice estimating and measuring with centimeters

How

- Make a record sheet like the one below.
- You and your child should estimate if your pencils are **shorter than** 15 centimeters (1.5 decimeters), **about** 15 cm long, or **longer than** 15 cm.
- Check the appropriate record sheet columns to indicate your estimates.
- Then measure the length of the pencils.
- Follow the same procedure for the other objects.
- Find more objects to estimate and measure. Are you both better at estimating now?

OBJECT	ESTIMATE			MEASUREMENT
	LESS THAN 15 cm.	ABOUT 15cm	GREATER THAN 15cm	
PENCIL	✓ DADS	✓ JOHNS		JOHNS – 12 cm DADS – 9 cm
BOOK				
TABLE				
FROM YOUR ELBOW TO YOUR WRIST				
THE LENGTH OF YOUR FOOT				

More Ideas

- To make the activity more challenging, only use objects that are close to 15 cm in length.
- Do the same activity for 12 inches (1 foot).

15 centimeter ruler

0 1 2 3 4 5 6 7 8 9 10 11 12 13 14 15

Fig. 2. Family Math activity

Community collaboration

Community collaboration refers to coordinating the work and resources of community businesses, agencies, colleges or universities, and other groups to enhance student learning, family practices, and school programs. This collaboration includes holding community meetings that not only inform the community about the mathematics programs in their schools but also allows mathematics educators to hear the needs of the community. Schools may also organize mathematics carnivals in which their students demonstrate mathematics projects and activities (e.g., running school stores; estimating impromptu calculations; and demonstrating on computers mathematics software, geometric constructions, and games of chance). These activities allow the community to become involved in the mathematics education of its young (see also Koes and Saab [1996, 118–21], for an example of a "mathematics olympics").

The business community can also take a more active role in mathematics education by offering financial or material support, such as purchasing computers, mathematics software, calculators, and mathematics manipulatives or donating restaurant menus and grocery flyers. In addition, local organizations may establish partnerships with schools so that students can spend a day at the particular business and observe how mathematics is applied in the real world. Moreover, individual employees can offer their support by volunteering to spend an hour a week at the school, tutoring students in mathematics.

Local colleges and universities can become involved, on the one hand, by providing intellectual and material support for mathematics teachers and by organizing professional-development activities. On the other hand, universities can offer events on campus that include field trips to mathematics or science departments and demonstrations of their laboratories. These activities—which are some of the many that support community collaboration—foster a reservoir of goodwill between schools and the community and, as a result, enhance the mathematical experiences of students.

Decision making

Decision making refers to parents' participation in school decisions, governance, and advocacy activities through committees, councils, school boards, and parent-teacher associations. Involvement in decision making is viewed by many to be the most empowering and productive type of parental involvement. However, it is also considered to be the most difficult and challenging type of involvement to organize and implement. This situation is particularly true for mathematics education because the mathematics community has made great efforts to enhance its professional status, and parental involvement in decision-making activities may be perceived as challenging the professional position of mathematics teachers and educators.

Nonetheless, as teachers, administrators, and parents become more comfortable with parental involvement in mathematics education, the role of parents in the schooling process can increase to include more central decision-making activities. This inclusion might involve giving parents a voice in decisions regarding mathematics curriculum, mathematics textbooks, forms of mathematics assessment, general policy, personnel, governance (including site-based management), and global reform issues. Schools that have taken this approach rely on various strategies to increase parental participation: membership of parents on the steering committee for a school's overall reform efforts, parental representation on every school committee, parent coordinators within the school, and parent-involvement cadres that focus on increasing the involvement of all parents (Comer 1980; Levin 1987). This inclusive approach to school decision making and parental involvement creates a sense of shared responsibility among parents, community members, teachers, administrators, and educators. In turn, this shared responsibility not only ensures that parents' values and interests are heard and respected but also fosters ownership and support for reform-based mathematics programs.

Closing Remarks

The school-mathematics-reform movement, guided by the NCTM's *Standards* documents, affects a variety of people in a variety of ways. Mathematics teachers and students face challenges as they plan and engage in activities that are student centered, set in meaningful contexts, and incorporate rich mathematical content in problem-solving situations. Administrators and postsecondary faculty are also challenged to support mathematics teachers' efforts as they continue to implement these reform-based visions of mathematics education. Central to the reform effort are the parents of these students who are experiencing this new vision of school mathematics and who are perhaps most affected by changes in mathematics content and pedagogy. These parents—parents who in the past have not been offered a formal role in the mathematics education of their children—are showing an increased interest in their children's mathematical experiences and are poised to affect the course of school mathematics reform. It is essential that parents and community members be involved in mathematics education so that they understand, support, and contribute to the teaching of school mathematics. The mathematics education community must make efforts to develop systematic programs for parental involvement so that all the people who have an interest in our students' mathematics development also have a role in which they can meaningfully participate.

References

Bloch, M. N., and R. B. Tabachnick. "Improving Parent Involvement as School Reform: Rhetoric or Reality?" In *Changing American Education: Recapturing the Past or Inventing the Future?*, edited by K. M. Borman and N. P. Greeman, 261–29. Albany: State University of New York Press, 1994.

Burrill, Gail. "President's Message: We Are Making Progress." *National Council of Teachers of Mathematics News Bulletin*, 3, May/June 1996.

Chavkin, Nancy F., ed. *Families and Schools in a Pluralistic Society*. Albany: State University of New York Press, 1993.

Clark, Reginald M. *Family Life and School Achievement: Why Poor Black Children Succeed and Fail*. Chicago: University of Chicago Press, 1983.

Comer, James P. *School Power: Implications of an Intervention Project*. New York: Free Press, 1980.

Comer, James P., and N. M. Haynes. *Summary of School Development Program Effects*. New Haven: Yale Child Study Center, 1992.

Delgado-Gaitan, Concha. *Literacy for Empowerment: The Role of Parents in Children's Education*. London: Falmer Press, 1990.

Epstein, Joyce L. "Theory to Practice: School and Family Partnerships Lead to School Improvement." In *School, Family and Community Interaction: A View from the Firing Lines*, edited by Cheryl L. Fagnano and Beverly Z. Werber, 39–52. Boulder, Colo.: Westview Press, 1994.

Filmore, Lily Wong. "Now or Later? Issues Related to the Early Education of Minority-Group Children." In *Early Childhood and Family Education: Analysis and Recommendations of the Council of Chief State School Officers*, 122–45. New York: Harcourt Brace Jovanovich, 1990.

Hall, Jane B., and Rita P. Acri. "A Fourth-Grade Family Math Night." *Teaching Children Mathematics* 2 (September 1995): 8–11.

Henderson, A. T., and N. Berla, eds. *A New Generation of Evidence: The Family Is Critical to Student Achievement*. National Committee for Citizens in Education, 1994.

Koes, Mary T., and Joy Faini Saab. "Where All Are Winners: A Mathematics Olympics for Parents, Students, and Teachers." *Teaching Children Mathematics* 3 (November 1996): 118–21.

Lareau, A. *Home Advantage: Social Class and Parental Intervention in Elementary Education.* London: Falmer Press, 1989.

Lazerick, Beth, and Judith Day Seidel. "Tech Time's News from the Net: Helping Your Child Learn Math." *Teaching Children Mathematics* 3 (November 1996): 141.

Levin, Henry M. "Accelerated Schools for Disadvantaged Students." *Educational Leadership* 44 (1987): 19–21.

Liontos, Lynn L. *At-Risk Families and Schools: Becoming Partners.* Eugene, Oreg.: ERIC Clearinghouse on Educational Management, 1992.

Madigan, T. J. "Parent Involvement and School Achievement." Paper presented at the annual meeting of the American Educational Research Association, New Orleans, Louisiana, 1994.

Moles, O. C. "Collaboration between Schools and Disadvantaged Parents: Obstacles and Openings." In *Families and Schools in a Pluralistic Society,* edited by Nancy F. Chavkin, 21–49. Albany: State University of New York Press, 1993.

National Council of Teachers of Mathematics (NCTM). *Curriculum and Evaluation Standards for School Mathematics.* Reston, Va.: NCTM, 1989.

———. *Professional Standards for Teaching Mathematics.* Reston, Va.: NCTM, 1991.

———. *Assessment Standards for School Mathematics.* Reston, Va.: NCTM, 1995.

National Parent-Teacher Association. *A Blueprint for Action: Parents and Community.* Washington, D.C.: American Association for the Advancement of Science, 1994.

Ogbu, John U. "Overcoming Racial Barriers to Equal Access." In *Access to Knowledge,* edited by John I. Goodlad, 59–90. New York: College Entrance Examination Board, 1990.

Peressini, Dominic. "Parents, Power, and the Reform of Mathematics Education: An Exploratory Analysis of Three Urban High Schools." *Urban Education* 31 (1996): 3–28.

———. "The Portrayal of Parents in the Reform of Mathematics Education: Locating the Context for Parent Involvement." *Journal for Research in Mathematics Education,* in press.

Price, Jack. "President's Report: Building Bridges of Mathematical Understanding for All Children." *Journal for Research in Mathematics Education* 27 (September 1996): 603–8.

Rich, Dorothy. *The Forgotten Factor in School Success: The Family.* Washington, D.C.: Home and School Institute, 1985.

Sarason, S. B. *Parental Involvement and the Political Principle.* San Francisco: Jossey-Bass, 1995.

Sattes, Beth D. *Parent Involvement: A Review of the Literature.* Charleston, W. V.: Appalachia Educational Laboratory, 1985.

Scott-Jones, D. "Families Influences on Cognitive Development and School Achievement." *Review of Research in Education* 11 (1984): 259–304.

Stenmark, Jean Kerr, Virginia Thompson, and Ruth Cossey. *Family Math.* Berkeley, Calif.: Lawrence Hall of Science, University of California at Berkeley, 1986.

Swap, Susan M. *Developing Home-School Partnerships.* New York: Teachers College Press, 1993.

United States Department of Education. *Goals 2000: A World-Class Education for Every Child.* Washington, D.C.: United States Government Printing Office, 1994.

No Kidding, My Mom's Got Homework?

Tuiren A. Bratina

The American public hears repeatedly that parents and guardians need to take a more active role in their children's education. The Carnegie Task Force (1989) recommends that families become reengaged in the education of their young adolescent children. Mathematics educators must promote practices that encourage involvement of those at home.

The Value of Parental Involvement

Research suggests that students' academic suc-cess improves with greater parental involvement (Epstein and Dauber 1991; Myers 1985). By working cooperatively with a parent as a partner, children develop better problem-solving skills. Some elementary school children in College Park, Maryland, were in a program called Math Pairs—Parents as Partners. They showed significantly greater improvement in problem-solving tasks as compared with those children who were not paired with a home partner (O'Connell 1992). Students' mathematical abilities also improve when students are able to discuss their thinking with a family member (Ford and Crew 1991; Leonard and Tracy 1993).

Another benefit of parental involve-

Tuiren Bratina teaches at the University of Northern Florida, Jacksonville, FL 32224. Her interests include developing a middle-level teacher-education program. The author would like to thank Sue O'Connell for her help in preparing this article.

ment is the close relationships that are formed when children and parents devote time together on school activities (Myers 1985). At the conclusion of a project in which parents and children played specially designed mathematical games, the researcher reported that "[parents] knew far more about their children's understanding of mathematics at the end of the project" (Tregaskis 1991, 15). A closer relationship may prove motivational in other ways, such as in increased homework-completion rates and better student attitudes about school and homework (Epstein et al. 1992). Parents who take the time to work with their children at home demonstrate the value they place on education.

A third reason to promote home involvement is that parents have the ability to help their children and thus become a valuable resource to the classroom teacher. Myers (1985) points out that parents can be trained for whatever task needs to be done. In fact, many successful parent-involvement programs incorporate workshops for training parents. The Math Pairs—Parents as Partners (O'Connell 1992), MAP (Monitoring Achievement in Pittsburgh)-AT-HOME (Weidman and LeMahieu 1985), and TIPS (Teachers Involve Parents in Schoolwork) (Epstein et al. 1992) programs focus much attention on training parents.

A Sample Program

The challenge to educators is designing programs that get parents

involved. Chris Potter, a sixth-grade teacher at Landmark Middle School in Jacksonville, Florida, found an effective method. She periodically sends worksheets home for parents and guardians to do with their children. The content relates to the mathematics that her students have already learned in class, so the worksheet's intent is for children to discuss methods and processes with their families. Students take the work to an adult in their home and sit and discuss the methods that are appropriate for solving the problem. Potter's assignments focus on real-life data, such as statistics, and on cartoons and articles that appear in the local newspaper (fig. 1). This homework not only reinforces the mathematics that her sixth graders are learning but has other benefits as well, such as the classroom discussion when students share with their classmates the different strategies that are used by various family members. Students also benefit from recognizing that learning is a lifelong pursuit and that families and extended families can learn together. One parent who was interviewed by a Jacksonville, Florida, television reporter said, "By working together we both learn" ("Top of the Class" 1993). Students like the idea of adults' doing homework, too. A typical response from students in Potter's class was, "No kidding, you mean my mom's got homework tonight? Wait 'til she hears this!"

Parents were enthusiastic about the assignments, too. "I even got letters back from several adults saying to keep *my* homework coming," Potter reported. One parent indicated with

THE LOCKHORNS

©1993 King Features Syndicate, Inc. World rights reserved.

"SO I MISSED ONE OF YOUR BIRTHDAYS IN 25 YEARS OF MARRIAGE. WHAT'S WRONG WITH A .980 BATTING AVERAGE?"

Fig. 1. If Leroy Lockhorn missed one of Loretta Lockhorn's birthdays in twenty-five years, what *would* his "batting average" be?

pleasure that she and her daughter talk about other things going on in her daughter's life after they sit together doing the schoolwork.

Potter reported that an overwhelming percent of families participated. She is in a fortunate position and can count on much support from those who are responsible for her students. But what about the child who does not live with an adult but who is eager to participate in this activity? This delicate situation requires a resourceful teacher who is able to identify alternative approaches. Capable people are available who are willing to help. For example, Mack (1992) suggests that the Distributive Education Clubs of America (DECA) has been successful when connecting businesspeople with parents and guardians to bring expertise into the classroom. Wonderful volunteers in such programs as the Big Brother and Big Sister organizations and the Boy Scouts and Girl Scouts could be of help. One can also solicit help from athletes, politicians, senior citizens, and church groups. It is wise to tap all these resources, as well as older siblings, aunts, uncles, or grandparents.

Tips for Involving Parents

To increase the effectiveness of efforts to get parents involved with

homework, consider some of the following tips:

1. Make sure parents understand the task. The first parent-teacher conference in the fall is a good time to explain the program. As mentioned previously, some programs offer workshops to train parents to become effectively involved. Telephone communications between the school and home have proved successful. For example, Cottle (1991) established an answering-machine message so that members from home could access information concerning homework. Both parents and students reported that this telephone communication system was helpful. Newsletters and letters are also a popular way to spread the word (Apelman and King 1993) (fig. 2). Regardless of the method of disseminating the information, make certain the directions are clear and easy to understand.

2. Keep the activities simple. Activities should *reinforce* or *enrich* classroom lessons. In the TIPS program, parents are *not* expected to teach school skills. The only requirement is that students talk to someone at home about the learning activity (Epstein et al. 1992). For example, one activity might involve the parents' taking children to the gasoline station, getting a receipt for a bill that shows the price of gasoline (e.g., $1.079 per gallon), and noticing the amount of gasoline purchased (e.g., 8.123 gallons). Student and parent then work together to determine the total cost of the gasoline and brainstorm other situations in which multiplying decimals is important. This activity connects decimals to a real-life example. (See **fig. 2**.)

3. Allow enough time for the assignment to be completed, such as two or three nights and possibly a weekend (Epstein et al. 1992). This time gives family members a better chance to

interact with their children on the homework. Activities should not create pressure for the parent or penalize a child if a parent is unable to help on one specific evening. For instance, if parents and children are to keep statistics for part of a basketball game, they need enough time to attend or watch a game. The busy schedules of parents should be a consideration. Be realistic about expectations.

4. Use school-home activities frequently and regularly for greatest impact (Epstein et al. 1992). "Teachers of any subject can design and assign homework in a way that requires students to interact with a parent about something interesting that they are learning in school" (Epstein and Dauber 1991, 300).

5. Design practical activities for all families. Costs should not be prohibitive. Learning experiences should not require too much time. If parents and their children are being asked to keep statistics on fifteen minutes of a basketball game, encourage them to attend a local event at school or at a parks-and-recreation facility. Whenever possible, give students resources to take home with them, such as charts, calculators, and newspapers.

6. Follow up by getting feedback from students and parents as well as administrators and others who can contribute good input. Use the results to improve your system.

Additional Parental-Involvement Ideas

Commercially produced and teacher-created games and take-home kits have also been successful materials in promoting home involvement in mathematics learning. Leonard and Tracy (1993) encourage using mathematically oriented games for middle school children. They have compiled a list of games, complete with costs, and have evaluated each game to determine which of the NCTM's *Curriculum and Evaluation Standards* (1989) are addressed when playing the games. For example, playing cards can be used to meet most of the

Dear Parents,

Have your children been talking about their most recent math study—calculating the rate of a car's gasoline consumption? In preparation for this assignment, we have been discussing the meaning of the term "miles per gallon": we have walked a mile, looked at gallon jugs and cans, and studied area maps to find familiar towns that are approximately thirty miles apart. The children are beginning to understand how much gasoline is used by a car that "gets" thirty miles per gallon (mpg).

We've practiced how to keep track of and calculate a car's mileage and gasoline consumption, and we've also talked about road and driving conditions that may influence gasoline consumption—on highways or in the city; on flat, hilly, paved, or gravel roads; in good or bad weather; in light or heavy traffic.

The children now need to practice in a real situation and are looking forward to keeping track of their family car's rate of gasoline consumption. I've enclosed a chart for you to use for this purpose, as well as directions that outline the method the students used when making these calculations in school. I hope they will be able to practice with you and that everyone will enjoy this family project. Records like these can be most useful when you take longer family trips, and your children will gain valuable skills keeping these records.

Good luck!

Name_____

GASOLINE CONSUMPTION

Date	Odometer Reading	Number of Miles Driven	Amount of Gasoline Used	Miles per Gallon	Cost of One Gallon	Total Cost	Driving Conditions

Fig. 2. Sample letter and chart (Apelman and King 1993)

standards, and a package usually costs about one dollar. Such games as Yahtzee, Life, Battleship, and Risk reinforce important mathematics skills. Tregaskis (1991) designed his own mathematical games for his students and their families. Joseph (1993) describes a project for involving family members with computer activities.

Creating specific boxes, take-home kits, or packs with mathematical materials and activity sheets has been successfully tried by several educators (Ford and Crew 1991; Franklin and Krebill 1993; O'Connell 1992) (figs. 2 and 3). TIPS-prototype mathematics activities are available for grades K–5 and contain good ideas for middle-grades homework (Epstein et al. 1992).

The numerous benefits of parental involvement include an increase in student achievement, a stronger parent-child relationship, and the pro-

gram's being an additional valuable resource to teachers. Programs can be implemented easily. A wide variety of parent-involvement programs exist that are dependent on students and their needs. Regardless of the type of program to be implemented, students, parents, and teachers will benefit from the home-school connection. Taking a step toward helping students' families become reengaged in their children's education will

Fig. 3. Students and parents are challenged by this problem from *The I Hate Mathematics! Book* (Burns 1975), which enriches probability lessons.

ultimately serve all concerned well in the future.

References

Apelman, Maja, and Julie King. *Exploring Everyday Math: Ideas for Students, Teachers, and Parents.* Portsmouth, N.H.: Heinemann Educational Books, 1993.

Burns, Marilyn. *The I Hate Mathematics! Book.* Boston: Little, Brown & Co., 1975.

Carnegie Council on Adolescent Development. *Turning Points: Preparing Youth for the Twenty-first Century.* New York: Carnegie Corporation of New York, 1989.

Cottle, William E. *Improving Communications between Parents and Teachers of Middle School Age Students by the Use of the Telephone and Other Techniques.* Ed. D. Practicum Report, Nova University, 1991. ERIC Document ED335616.

Epstein, Joyce L., and Susan L. Dauber. "School Programs and Teacher Practices of Parent Involvement in Inner-City Elementary and Middle Schools." *Elementary School Journal* 91(January 1991):289–305.

Epstein, Joyce L., et al. *Manual for Teachers: Teachers Involve Parents in Schoolwork (TIPS). Language Arts and Science/Health. Interactive Homework in the Middle Grades.* Baltimore Md.: Johns Hopkins University, 1992.

Ford, Marilyn Sue, and Caroline Gibson Crew. "Table-Top Mathematics—a Home-Study Program for Early Childhood." *Arithmetic Teacher* 38 (April 1991): 6–12.

Franklin, Joyce, and Joyce Krebill. "Teacher to Teacher: Take-Home Kits." *Arithmetic Teacher* 40 (April 1993): 442–48.

Joseph, Helen. "Teaching Mathematics with Technology: Build Parental Support for Mathematics with Family Computers." *Arithmetic Teacher* 40 (March 1993): 412–15.

Leonard, Lisa M., and Dyanne M. Tracy. "Using Games to Meet the Standards for Middle School Students." *Arithmetic Teacher* 40 (May 1993): 499–503.

Mack, Maureen D. "Changing Families—Changing Middle Schools." *Middle School Journal* 24 (September 1992): 55–60.

Myers, John W. *Involving Parents in Middle Level Education.* Columbus, Ohio: National Middle School Association, 1985.

National Council of Teachers of Mathematics. *Curriculum and Evaluation Standards for School Mathematics.* Reston, Va.: The Council, 1989.

O'Connell, Susan R. "Math Pairs—Parents as Partners." *Arithmetic Teacher* 40 (September 1992): 10–12.

"Top of the Class." WTLV-Channel 12 News. Jacksonville, Fla.: 3 December 1993.

Tregaskis, Owen. "Parents and Mathematical Games." *Arithmetic Teacher* 38 (March 1991): 14–16.

Weidman, John C., and Paul LeMahieu. "Parent Involvement in Children's Out-of-School Learning: The MAP-AT-HOME Program." Paper presented at the Annual Meeting of the American Sociological Association, 27 August 1985. ERIC Document ED262296.

Parents and Children Doing Mathematics at Home

Marlene Kliman

How can parents help their children be enthusiastic about mathematics? What is the mathematical equivalent of reading out loud to children every day? How can teachers support parents in doing mathematics with their children in engaging and productive ways?

Ongoing parental involvement in mathematics—as in any subject—can provide a solid foundation for children's learning and attitudes (Peressini 1998; Mokros 1996; Apelman and King 1993). When parents maintain high expectations for their children's performance in mathematics, regularly do mathematical activities with their children, and display a positive attitude toward mathematics, children benefit. They are more likely to feel confident in their abilities; to enjoy and learn more from the mathematics that they experience at school; and to develop a sense of the richness, usefulness, and pervasiveness of mathematics.

This article offers ideas to help parents integrate mathematics into their family lives in ways that are consistent with the NCTM's Standards (NCTM 1989). These ideas were gathered from teachers in a wide range of school settings. As teachers made changes in their mathematics teaching, they kept parents informed and enlisted their support. They let parents know what was happening in class and asked them to help with homework. Some teachers also encouraged families to do mathematics together regularly and experience mathematics as an engaging family activity.

Getting Started

To succeed in integrating mathematics into daily family life, parents need to understand how doing mathematics at home can foster children's learning, and they need appealing and manageable activity ideas. The following paragraphs offer some suggestions for teachers to help parents get started.

Begin early in the year

Launch the idea of doing mathematics at home near the start of the school year so that parents have plenty of time to try a range of activities, to share ideas with one another, and to reflect on their children's mathematics learning at home and at school. A parent night or conference is an ideal time to introduce the idea; if that idea is not possible, send a letter home. In one district, the mathematics coordinator sent a letter to parents about a month after school began, explaining the importance of regularly doing mathematics at home and offering a few activities for families to try. Teachers followed up in their classrooms with activity ideas and resource lists sent home throughout the year.

Draw a connection to the family's role in literacy

Most parents are familiar with the importance of reading to their children regularly; teachers may find it helpful to draw a parallel between supporting children's literacy and mathematics at home. Ask parents to consider the ways that they support their children's reading and writing throughout the day and give some typical examples. For instance, many parents point out familiar words on package labels to beginning readers, listen while their children read aloud, encourage their children to write thank-you notes, and make up stories and rhymes with their children. Explain that encouraging children's mathematics skills is similar to encouraging their language skills. Just as many opportunities arise for supporting children's literacy throughout the day, so are many opportunities possible to enjoy mathematics together.

Share anecdotes

One first-grade teacher sparked parents' awareness of mathematics in everyday situations by sharing anecdotes about their children's mathematical thinking outside of mathematics class. At parent conferences early in the year, the teacher cited examples from the classroom—children figuring out how many minutes remained until lunch time; reasoning about spatial relationships when doing a construction project; and combining, comparing, and categorizing as they discussed their collections of toy animals, toy cars, and shells. For each example, she clearly explained the mathematics that the child was doing, such as counting, adding, and working with properties of geometric shapes.

Providing Activity Ideas

After you have introduced the idea of integrating more mathematics into family life, offer some examples based on familiar situations that are rich with mathematical opportunities. Some teachers periodically send home a letter with activity ideas (see **fig. 1**); others append various activity ideas to each issue of their regular classroom newsletters. The following paragraphs offer some useful ideas for developing letters to send home.

Group suggestions around family situations or events

Most parents will find it easier to integrate mathematics into family time by building on activities that they already do. Group your suggestions according to everyday situations, events, and places rather than content areas. Emphasize contexts in which mathematics arises to show parents and children that mathematics is an integral part of everyday life. The letter in figure 1 suggests integrating mathematics into family meal time. Some other everyday contexts for activities follow. See NCTM (1998) and Mokros (1996) for more ideas.

1. *Story time.* Reading together is a wonderful way to explore ideas with children, including mathematical ideas. Many parents naturally pause to ask about characters, objects, and events: "Why do you think Chi-Hoon left the party? What do you think will happen next?" Parents can also include questions about counting; comparing; and finding totals and differences, shapes, and measurements. For instance, they might ask how many butterflies are in a picture and whether more are likely to be seen on the next page. How many more gold coins does a character need to buy a magic key? How many things shaped like triangles are on the page? Parents can also involve children in estimating amounts and sizes: "It says that this dinosaur was about twenty-five feet long and seven feet high. Would it fit in this room? In our apartment? How could we find out?"

Almost any children's book offers

some mathematical ideas to discuss. Parents can also explore the wide range of children's mathematical literature, including stories with mathematical themes, stories that contain logical puzzles, and stories in which characters use mathematics to help solve everyday problems. See McCarty (1998), Bresser (1995), and Burns (1992) for recommendations of excellent children's mathematical literature.

2. *Outdoors.* Just as many mathematical ideas can be explored in storybooks, so are many mathematical concepts found in the world outside. As parents spend time with their children in the neighborhood and backyard and on the playground, they can find things to count, compare, and tally: "How many windows does this house have? How many more windows does it have than our house? Which window in our house is the longest?"

Measuring and comparing arise naturally as children work on their athletic skills—can your child jump higher, skip rope longer, or run faster than he or she could last year or last month? Parents can help young children use rulers, tape measures, or stopwatches to figure out just how high, how fast, or how long is a certain measure and to keep track of and compare progress. Older children can do more measuring, timing, keeping track, and comparing by themselves. They can also investigate questions that involve rates, speeds, and averages. For instance, children who are interested in running might keep track of their running times or speeds, compute averages, and graph their progress.

3. *On the road.* Car or bus trips are wonderful times to explore numbers, shapes, and counting. One activity appropriate for a wide range of ages is a mathematical scavenger hunt. Family members take turns finding something to watch for, such as a truck with eight wheels, a speed limit over thirty-five, a house number between 995 and 1195, or a road sign shaped like a square. While a parent is driving, the children can keep their eyes open!

Another car or bus activity that is fun involves estimating, collecting data, and keeping track. Children can make predictions about how many dogs they will see; whether more traffic lights or stop signs will be found; or whether more billboards on the route will advertise food, clothing, or entertainment. During the trip, they can count and keep track, using tallies, numbers, pictures, or charts. After the trip, parents can work with children to explore the data: "How many more stop signs than traffic lights did you see on the way to school? Why do you think that more stop signs were found? Do you think that it would be true for any road? Let's count again when we go to the grocery store tomorrow." See figure 2 for data about dogs that two children gathered on car trips.

4. *Household chores.* Sometimes asking a mathematical question or two can make children more enthusiastic about participating in household chores. Parents can engage children in matching, sorting, and counting as they do the laundry: "I wonder who has the most clothing in this load of laundry? Let's sort it to find out." Household chores can also provide a context for estimating and counting large quantities as children organize their belongings: "How many books do you have? About twenty-five? One hundred? One thousand? Let's count them as we arrange them neatly on your bookshelf." Children can also get involved in estimating sizes and measurements: "Here's one folded towel. How high would a pile of ten of them be? Up to your knees? Up to your waist? Over your head? Let's fold these towels and see."

Other chores can involve measuring quantities, reading tables and charts, and working with fractions. In one family, children worked on mathematics every day as they fed a kitten. They used a measuring cup to find the right amount of kitten chow each day, usually an amount involving fractions, and they kept track of the kitten's age in weeks so that they could be sure to

give it enough food as it grew. The parents used the chart on the back of the food bag, listing the amount of food for the age in weeks, as a basis for talking about when and how the kitten's food needs would change.

Offer ideas on activities for the whole family

Although you will probably emphasize activities that are appropriate for the age range in your class, you should also provide ideas for parents to adapt activities or ask questions that involve the entire family. Making sense of bar graphs in the newspaper, for example, might be more appropriate for children in the middle or upper-elementary grades. Younger children in the family can participate, however, by reading numbers on the graph; determining which bar in the graph is highest; or counting how many bars are on the graph. Some teachers label their proposed activity ideas with approximate grade ranges, as shown in figure 1.

Draw connections to content from school

From time to time, suggest family activities that extend or support the content that you are working on in class. One kindergarten class was working on a pattern unit, so the teacher asked families to look for patterns in clothes as they sorted laundry. When the class was working on geometry, the teacher asked that families investigate roof, chimney, and window shapes in the neighborhood. These activities were not intended to replace homework assignments that helped children practice specific skills and concepts, but served as broader questions that the whole family could explore.

Help parents share with each other

Solicit from parents ideas on mathematics activities that they have tried at home, and ask them to write down activities and anecdotes to share with others. Encourage parents who have a little extra time, writing expertise, or computer experience to assume responsibility for family letters by gathering activity ideas or producing the letters. In one classroom, a different family took responsibility for the mathematics letter each month. The activities in figure 1 were compiled in this manner. In another classroom, several bilingual parents volunteered to translate letters for parents who spoke little or no English.

Offer ideas for optional resources

Teachers should emphasize that families can do a great deal of mathematics without special materials but that some families may have the time and interest to investigate other mathematical resources. These resources might include books on mathematics teaching and learning (e.g., Hartog et al. [1998]; Kanter [1993]; Mokros et al. [1995]); children's mathematical literature; manipulatives, such as pattern blocks and geoboards; parent mathematics education Web sites, such as the site sponsored by the U.S. Department of Education at **www.ed.gov/pubs/parents/Math**; and mathematical games, software, and other activities. Parents, other teachers, or school librarians might be able to help compile a parent resource list. Parents can help by annotating the list with summaries of resources that they know about and descriptions of how they have used these materials with their children. Some parents might also be willing to lend their own books or games to other families. On your resource list, note which items that parents can preview or borrow from your classroom or school library, which they might be able to borrow from a public library, and which they might need to purchase.

Providing Ongoing Support

Parents will benefit from continued opportunities to share suggestions for, and experiences with, doing mathematics at home; to discuss what they

notice about their children's thinking and learning; to make connections between mathematics at home and mathematics in the classroom; and to talk about changes in their own views of mathematics. The following are some ways that teachers can help.

Keep communication open

Check with parents about mathematics at home from time to time—when you see them at parent night, parent conferences, or other school events. Ask parents about their experiences of doing mathematics with their children and relate anecdotes about their children's mathematical thinking that you have noticed outside mathematics class. You can also help parents share their experiences with their peers. If parents visit your classroom on a regular basis, devote a corner of a bulletin board to mathematics at home and invite parents to post notes about their successes and challenges. In one school, a teacher helped a group of parent volunteers take responsibility for communicating with other parents about mathematics at home. The teacher led a few sessions on mathematics activities for families, then the volunteers encouraged other parents to telephone them with questions and ideas about doing mathematics at home.

Draw connections to teaching and learning at school

As parents become engaged in investigating mathematics with their children, they not only support their children's learning but may also begin to experience mathematics in new ways themselves. When you speak with parents, look for opportunities to draw connections between the experiences that they report having at home and the approaches that you are using in your classroom. One teacher regularly encouraged parents to listen carefully to their children's explanations when solving problems and offered such reminders as these: "Whether you are working on homework or just doing mathematics together at home, if your children get the wrong answer, the

first thing to do is ask them how they solved the problem." She found that as parents explored mathematics with their children in a relaxed and informal way, they began to appreciate the importance of communicating mathematical thinking. Her reminders helped parents recognize that explaining strategies for solving problems is just as important when children are working on homework as it is when they are doing mathematics in class. Another teacher found that when parents became aware of their children's strategies for solving computation problems in everyday life and began to reflect on their own mental arithmetic strategies, they were more supportive of her approach to teaching computation, which involved children inventing their own strategies.

Encourage parents to find their own approaches

In your letters to, and other communications with, parents, emphasize that the activities you suggest are just a sampling of the many ways that parents can share mathematics in everyday life with their children. As parents go through the day, they will find many other situations that are rich with opportunities for mathematics, such as estimating how many cookies are needed for a party, measuring cloth for a sewing project, counting the number of days until a birthday, figuring out the time difference before calling a relative in another time zone, or determining the right change in the grocery store. When parents recognize these mathematical opportunities, they can draw the experiences out for their children by asking a question or two, then listening while their children explain their thinking. Parents can also look for opportunities to demonstrate ways that they themselves use mathematics as they go about the day. They might try talking out loud about the process of balancing a checkbook or tripling a recipe. Even if children are too young to understand the details, they will see and hear their parents using mathematics to solve important problems, taking time to

Dear Families:

This month's letter is on Meal Time Math—quick ways to do math with your children as you plan, cook, serve, and eat meals. Each idea includes questions tried by parents in our class and a grade range for the activities.

How much food should we make? Ask your children to help you figure out how much food is needed for a meal, a set of lunch boxes, or a party. They'll practice counting, adding, or multiplying.

- How many sandwiches do we need if each adult eats two, Ana eats half, and the other children eat one? (pre-K–2)
- We need enough soup for three meals. Will we have enough if we double this recipe? What if we triple it? (2–6)

What do we need for this recipe? Involve your children in reading and adjusting recipes as you prepare meals. The work involves measurement, fractions, volume, and ratios.

- Can you measure out exactly three-fourths of a cup of flour? (pre-K–2)
- I'm going to make one-third of this recipe. It calls for twelve carrots. How many do we need? (2–4)
- For this punch mix, we need two ounces of lemon juice per cup of soda. How much lemon juice will we need if we use a gallon of soda? Can you find a container that holds a gallon? (2–6)

What do we need to set the table? Enlist the help of young children when setting the table to give them practice counting and combining things that come in two and threes.

- Put out a knife, fork, and spoon for everyone. How many pieces of silverware did you put out? (pre-K–2)
- We have two guests. How many plates do we need? How many spoons, if everyone gets two? (pre-K–2)

What's fair? Next time your children clamor for fair division of a favorite food, invite them to propose their own solutions! For food that comes in small pieces, children practice with counting, arithmetic, or fractions. For food that comes in pans or large pieces, children work with shapes and area.

- How can we divide these cherries fairly among three children? (pre-K–4)
- What's the fairest way to share these three brownies among the four of us? (2–4)
- How can we split up this tree-shaped pan of Jell-O so that everyone gets the same amount? (2–6)

A miniproject: How far to our table? As children explore where their food comes from, they work with distance units, scale, and maps. (All ages)

- Predict which food in the meal comes from farthest away and which comes from closest to home.
- Check product labels or stickers on fruit and vegetables for places of origin.
- Use maps to find out how many miles the food has traveled to get to your home.

Fig. 1. Sample "Math at Home" letter

work through ideas, checking their reasoning, and even finding and correcting mistakes.

The Most Important Message to Parents: You Can Make a Difference!

Teachers can help parents integrate more mathematics into their family lives in a number of ways, including sending out two or three sets of activity ideas during the school year, providing regular newsletters and resource lists, holding parent meetings, and collaborating with active groups of parent volunteers. Generally, the more engaged and interested the parental community is, the more successful the efforts will

that they *can* play a dynamic role in helping their children develop skills and interest in mathematics, confidence in their mathematical abilities, and positive attitudes toward mathematics. Assure parents that they do not have to be mathematical experts or enthusiasts to help their children. All adults—whatever their backgrounds—use mathematics in a variety of situations every day. By involving children in some of these situations, several times a day or just once a week, parents help their children view mathematics as a meaningful, natural part of everyday life, a tool for solving important and relevant problems, and an entertaining way to spend family time.

References

Apelman, Maya, and Julie King. *Exploring Everyday Math: Ideas for Students, Teachers, and Parents.* Portsmouth, N.H.: Heinemann, 1993.

Bresser, Rusty. *Math and Literature (Grades 4–6).* White Plains, N.Y.: Math Solutions Publications, 1995.

Burns, Marilyn. *Math and Literature (K–3).* White Plains, N.Y.: Math Solutions Publications, 1992.

Hartog, Martin, Maria Diamantis, and Patricia Brosnan. "Doing Mathematics with Your Child." *Teaching Children Mathematics* 4 (February 1998): 326–30.

Kanter, Patsy. *Helping Your Child Learn Math.* Lexington, Mass.: D. C. Heath & Co., 1993.

McCarty, Diane. "Books + Manipulatives + Families = A Mathematics Lending Library." *Teaching Children Mathematics* 4 (February 1998): 368–75.

Mokros, Jan. *Beyond Facts and Flashcards: Exploring Math with Your Kids.* Portsmouth, N.H.: Heinemann, 1996.

Mokros, Jan, Susan Jo Russell, and Karen Economopoulos. *Beyond Arithmetic: Changing Mathematics in the Elementary Classroom.* Palo Alto, Calif.: Dale Seymour Publications, 1995.

National Council of Teachers of Mathematics (NCTM). *Curriculum and Evaluation Standards for School Mathematics.* Reston, Va.: NCTM, 1989.

———. "Focus Issue: Beyond the Classroom: Linking Mathematics Learning with Parents, Communities, and Business and Industry." *Teaching Children Mathematics* 4 (February 1998).

Peressini, Dominic. "What's All the Fuss about Involving Parents in Mathematics Education?" *Teaching Children Mathematics* 4 (February 1998): 320–25.

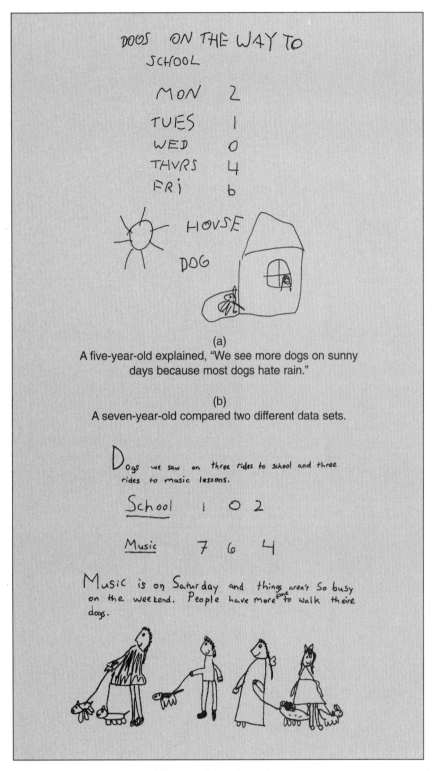

(a)
A five-year-old explained, "We see more dogs on sunny days because most dogs hate rain."

(b)
A seven-year-old compared two different data sets.

Fig. 2. Children's data gathered on car trips

be to involve the parents in doing mathematics with their children. Although some parents need just a few activity ideas to get going, others gain confidence and motivation from sharing ideas with their peers and need support in finding playful ways to do mathematics with their children.

No matter what kind of support you have available in your own classroom and community, perhaps the most important message to give to parents is

Reversing the Trend: Latino Families in Real Partnerships with Schools

Yolanda De La Cruz

Señor Lopez walked up to the project director after the last mathematics class and said, "De todos los años que he tenido hijos en estas escuelas, esta es la primera vez que me han tratado con tanta dignidad" (In all the years I have had children attend these schools, this is the first time that I have been treated with so much dignity).

Involving parents in their children's learning has been recognized as necessary and important by scholars who contributed to several reports on the nation's schools (De La Cruz, in press; Epstein and Becker 1982; Epstein 1983). The recommendation reflects the consistent findings in social science research that children have an added advantage in school when their parents encourage and support schooling.

Latino families are growing in numbers; currently they compose the largest minority group in the Southwest and have been visibly transforming culture and society (Takaki 1996). These families are seeking ways to improve their status in the United States and look to the educational process as a way of achieving this goal (Khisty and Becker

1990; Secada and De La Cruz 1996). By including them in real partnerships with schools, we can help them reach these goals.

This article outlines a research-based model for greater family involvement among Latino families in the area of mathematics. The

Yolanda De La Cruz, ydelacruz@asu.edu, teaches mathematics education courses at Arizona State University West, Phoenix, AZ 85069. Her research interests include working with teachers, families, and community organizations to develop mathematical concepts.

Edited by Tad Watanabe, Towson State University, Towson, MD 21204.

Children's Math Worlds Family Connection (CMWFC), is a component of a reform-mathematics curriculum called Children's Math Worlds (CMW), which was developed for first through third grades under the leadership of Karen C. Fuson at Northwestern University. The curriculum was developed over the past seven years, initially in urban Latino classrooms, but more recently in a range of other classrooms. The CMWFC component was directed by Yolanda De La Cruz at Arizona State University West and has been under development for three years.

Formal assessments were conducted of the mathematical understandings of various classes of urban children learning from our pedagogy (Fuson, Smith, and Lo Cicero 1997; Fuson 1996; Fuson 1998). Although more than 90 percent of our urban CMW children met federal guidelines for the free-lunch program, they considerably outperformed heterogeneous and middle-class samples of United States children who received traditional mathematics instruction. On many items, they outperformed children from Taiwan and United States children using the reform curriculum Everyday Mathematics (UCSMP 1998); and on some tasks, they equaled or exceeded the performance of Japanese children. On standardized tests, 90 percent of the urban children scored at grade level on computation and 65 percent on problem solving. Class means on overall mathematics scores were above grade level, some children scored three years above grade level, and no child scored more than one year below grade level. The results for suburban children were even stronger. The usual suburban-urban gap still existed but was smaller on some items.

Factors Affecting Latino Children's School Achievement

Several factors affect Latino children's school achievement (fig. 1). Often, traditional curricula do not offer enough

Four areas affect the mathematics learning of Latino students and prevent many of them from gaining access to this knowledge.

- Traditional curricula often leave gaps in conceptual understanding.
- Reform-based-mathematics instruction requires facility with oral and written English.
- Communication with limited-English-speaking parents is difficult.
- School programs often fail to include families in a teaching partnership.

Fig. 1

steps to help students with limited-English-speaking ability build better conceptual understanding. These students, therefore, fall farther and farther behind, leaving many of them with large knowledge gaps.

As more school districts require teachers to implement reform mathematics curricula, little support is offered in helping them develop strategies for new demands placed on their teaching. For example, teachers are finding that reform-based-mathematics instruction places more demands on facility with oral and written English. They do not have the strategies, however, that enable them to work more effectively with their limited-English-language students.

Many parents of Latino students either speak no English or are limited-English speakers; thus, communication between parents and teachers is not simple. Teachers express deep concern that not enough family participation occurs among Latino families, but they do not know how to develop partnerships with these families. More support is needed to help teachers overcome barriers that prevent them from building partnerships with the families of their students.

True partnerships with Latino families will result when more emphasis is placed on ascertaining their needs and convenient times for them to attend programs to acquire resources to help their children. Communication and language barriers must be overcome before any true partnership can result.

Families must be treated with the dignity that they deserve, and both teachers and parents must make an effort to develop and nurture partnerships that can reverse the trend of Latino underachievement in our schools.

CMWFC Approaches to These Issues

School reform programs are often developed without sufficient attention to how to attain the academic goals required for success among Latino and other linguistic-minority and ethnic-minority students. Several approaches helped to make the CMWFC successful in meeting the needs of Latino families. In the CMWFC, we asked parents what they needed to be able to help their children in mathematics. Print communication was always done in both Spanish and English. We sent surveys home with children and made follow-up calls to parents who had not responded to the survey. We found that parents wanted to learn to help their children at home but did not think that they had enough mathematics knowledge to help their children in grades 1 through 3.

We sent activity booklets home to families for each grade level, first through third, containing activities and games that reinforce school learning. The booklets were available to families throughout the school year. Figure 2 and figure 3 are examples of some of the information contained in these booklets. These games and activities reinforced the mathematics curriculum being taught in the school.

Families were invited to attend two workshops during the school year to help them improve their mathematics knowledge. These sessions were scheduled for parents with or without their children in attendance. In Illinois, we found that families preferred to bring their children to these workshops. The classes were given for parents first while children attended a separate program. After the first hour, the children joined their parents for the remainder of the workshop. These parents remarked that they felt more

How Many Pennies Did I Hide?

Materials:
1 penny strip

Players:
2 players

Purpose/mathematics skills practiced:
To learn which pairs of numbers make 10

Rules of the game:
A penny strip is laid penny side up in front of the two players. One player covers a number of pennies in the penny strip with a hand or a piece of cardboard and asks his or her partner, "How many pennies did I hide?" The partner has to figure out how many were covered and then checks the answer by uncovering the hidden pennies. If the partner gets it right, she or he gets a point.

Children take turns being the one to hide the pennies in the penny strip.

How many pennies did I hide?

Harder variation: When your child is good at this game, she or he can figure out how many pennies are covered. In this version, your child cannot see the penny strip. She or he has to do it with eyes closed! Ask, "I have four pennies left. How many did I hide?" or "I hid six pennies. How many did I have left?"

This game will help your child learn combinations of 10.

Fig. 2

¿Cuántos Centavos Escondí?

Materiales:
1 tira de centavos

Jugadores:
2 jugadores

Objetivo/Habilidades de matemáticas que se necesitan:
Aprender cuáles pares de números hacen 10

Reglas del juego:
Una tira de centavos se coloca con los centavos boca arriba frente a dos jugadores. Un jugador cubre un número de centavos en la tira de centavos (con la mano o una hoja de cartón), y le pregunta a su compañero "¿Cuántos centavos escondí?" El compañero tiene que comprender cuántos estaban escondidos y luego comprueba la respuesta decubriendo los centavos cubiertos. Si tiene razón, recibe un punto.

Los niños se turnan para ser el que cubre los centavos en la tira de centavos.

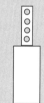

¿Cuántos centavos escondí?

Variación más difícil: Cuando su niño hace bien este juego, puede comprender cuántos centavos están cubiertos. No puede ver la tira de centavos. ¡Tiene que hacerlo con los ojos cerrados! Pregunte Ud, "Me quedan 4 centavos. ¿Cuántos cubrí?" o "Cubrí 6 centavos. ¿Cuántos me quedaron?"

Esto ayudará a su niño a aprender las combinaciones de 10.

Fig.3

confident once they had successfully done the activities without their children. We gave the mathematics workshops at times that were best for parents, as determined by the survey responses. We found that in both Illinois and Arizona, families preferred late-afternoon and weekend mathematics workshops. In Illinois, one hundred families attended the mathematics classes with their children, even in –43-degree-wind-chill weather.

Families viewed pilot videotapes, available in both English and Spanish, showing them how to do the mathematics activities. Families who attended the workshops checked out the videotapes from the school library whenever they wanted to review how to do the activities.

CMWFC offered workshops for teachers interested in gaining more family support. Teachers were given information on how to respect the needs of parents and how to treat them with the dignity they deserve. Eleven teachers attended the classes because their prior efforts had failed to produce family involvement. They found that sending letters home in both Spanish and English and making follow-up telephone calls made a great difference in gaining family support. When classes were scheduled at times that parents had requested, teachers were pleasantly surprised by the overwhelming parental response. Parents remarked that they had never been given a choice of times for school-related activities. They felt like real partners in the learning and teaching of their children.

Participants' Responses

Parents were asked to give written or oral evaluations after the workshops. The following outcomes are indicative of their responses.

- One father worked at night, and he was accustomed to sleeping in the late afternoon. But he decided instead to attend with his wife the mathematics classes offered through CMWFC so that they could both help their children with homework.

- One mother said that in Mexico, teaching was customarily left for the teacher. Here in the United States, she learned that teachers expect parents' help with homework.

- Another couple attended because they liked the games that their child was bringing home and wanted to learn how to play them.

- Many parents appreciated that only inexpensive materials were needed to play the games and activities.

Teachers were asked whether they noticed any differences due to the CMWFC workshops. Teachers replied that some of the parents approached them for various reasons related to mathematics homework, something that had not happened in the past. Typically, many Latino parents would not think of contacting their children's teachers, but because these parents participated in CMWFC, they felt comfortable enough to do so.

Future Directions

We are in the process of developing a series of home videotapes showing parents how to play various activities and games with their children. More games and activities are being developed to reinforce school mathematics learning in the home. Teachers are making their own videotapes to address particular needs of their Latino students' parents. They tape students as they explain a method or procedure so that parents gain more effective ways of helping their children. These videotapes explain to parents how to focus on the process instead of just on getting the correct answer. They give guidelines and sample questions that parents can use for this process.

Various community organizations have expressed an interest in expanding the program. Parents will be trained to help facilitate workshops for families. Teachers who are currently involved will train parents for future CMWFC workshops. Parent and teacher manuals for conducting workshops are under development. These manuals will describe how to meet teachers' and parents' expectations.

We are confident that these efforts to expand the program will help more schools and Latino families develop true partnerships.

References

De La Cruz, Yolanda. "A Model of Tutoring That Helps Students Gain Access to Mathematical Competence." In *Changing the Faces of Mathematics: Perspectives on Latinos*, edited by Luis Ortiz-Franco. Reston, Va.: National Council of Teachers of Mathematics, 1999.

Epstein, Joyce L. *Effects on Parents of Teacher Practices of Parent Involvement: Report 346*. Baltimore, Md.: Center for Social Organization of Schools, Johns Hopkins University, 1983.

Epstein, Joyce L., and Henry J. Becker. "Teachers' Reported Practices of Parent Involvement: Problems and Possibilities." *Elementary School Journal* 83 (1982): 103–13.

Fuson, Karen C. "Latino Children's Construction of Arithmetic Understanding in Urban Classrooms That Support Thinking." Paper presented at the annual meeting of the American Educational Research Association, New York, April 1996.

———. "Performance of Suburban CMW Children." Unpublished data, 1998.

Fuson, Karen C., Steven T. Smith, and Ana Marie Lo Cicero. "Supporting Latino First Graders' Ten-Structured Thinking in Urban Classrooms." *Journal for Research in Mathematics Education* 28 (December 1997): 738–60.

Khisty, Lena Licon, and Deborah Becker. "Speaking Mathematically in Bilingual Classrooms: An Exploratory Study of Teacher Discourse." In *Proceedings of the Fourteenth International Conference for the Psychology of Mathematics Education*, vol. 3, edited by G. Booker, P. Cobb, and T. Mendicutti, 105–12. Mexico City: CONTACYT, 1990.

Secada, Walter, and Yolanda De La Cruz. "Teaching Mathematics for Understanding to Bilingual Students." In *Children of la Frontera*, edited by J. LeBlanc Flores, 285–308. Charleston, W.V.: ERIC Clearinghouse on Rural Education and Small Schools, 1996.

Takaki, Ronald. "A Different Mirror." In *Color Class Identity: The New Politics of Race*, edited by J. Arthur and A. Shapario. Boulder, Colo.: University of Colorado Press, 1996.

University of Chicago School Mathematics Project (USCMP). *Everyday Mathematics*. Chicago: Everyday Learning Corp., 1998.

For more information on CMWFC, please contact Yolanda De La Cruz, ydelacruz@asu.edu, ASU West, College of Education, P.O. Box 37100, Phoenix, AZ 85069-7100.

The research reported in this article was supported by the National Science Foundation (NSF) under grant no. RED 935373, the Spencer Foundation, and the James S. McDonnell Foundation. The opinions expressed in this article are those of the author and do not necessarily reflect the views of the NSF, the Spencer Foundation, or the James S. McDonnell Foundation.

Want to drop mathematics? Consider the following questions and answers:

1. What percent of parents have never been informed about the decisions their children must make about future math courses and the implications? *Answer:* 93 percent

2. More than half of all students in grades 5 to 11 plan to drop math as soon as it is not required. What percent of African American students plan to drop mathematics and science at the first opportunity? *Answer:* 63 percent. For Latino and American Indian students, 60 percent and 58 percent, respectively.

3. What percent of minority students nationwide graduate from high school with the prerequisite mathematics and science courses necessary to begin an engineering or other science-based college major? *Answer:* 6 percent. For nonminority students, 12 percent.

4. What percent of students in grades 5–8 say their friends or significant adults in their lives have discouraged them from succeeding in math courses? *Answer:* 19 percent by friends, 17 percent by parents or guardians, 13 percent by other family members, and 15 percent by teachers.

Adapted from Virginia Thompson and Karen Mayfield Ingram, *Family Math—the Middle Years: Algebraic Reasoning and Number Sense* (Berkeley, Calif.: Lawrence Hall of Science, University of California at Berkeley, 1999). Original source from Robert Leitman, Katherine Binns, and Akhil Unni, "Uninformed Decisions: A Survey of Children and Parents about Math and Science," *NACME Research Letter* 5, no. 1, June 1995.

PARENTS

A READY RESOURCE

Sue Goldstein and Frances A. Campbell

I never seem to reach every student when I am teaching mathematics." "There is never enough time for practicing mathematics skills." These laments by typical elementary school teachers are both real and abundant. Teachers would love to have more time and more help to work with students individually on developing and mastering mathematics skills. Involving parents in working with their children in mathematics is a ready method of obtaining an extra resource for teachers when individualizing mathematics instruction.

In a large survey of how teachers involve parents in education, Epstein and Becker (1982) reported that only 35 percent of first-grade teachers and 20 percent of fifth-grade teachers actually promoted the use of informal learning activities to be carried out by parents. These authors pointed out that although teachers often questioned whether the time required to develop these kinds of activities was worth the trouble, teachers in fact rarely evaluated the effectiveness of parent-involvement activities on students' achievement. Researchers have reported that such activities do have positive effects. Having parents participate in their children's education can

Sue Goldstein is interested in all aspects of parental involvement in their children's education. She teaches at Frank Porter Graham Child Development Center of the University of North Carolina at Chapel Hill, Chapel Hill, NC 27599. Frances Campbell is coordinator of psychoeducational services at the same school. She is interested in intervention programs to enhance the success of disadvantaged students in school.

increase students' achievement (Bodner-Johnson 1986; Bronfenbrenner 1975; Grimmet and McCoy 1980; Kroth and Scholl 1978) and promote a more positive student attitude toward education (Glass 1978; Hayes, Cunningham, and Robinson 1977; Teller 1975).

This article highlights a study of educational intervention in the elementary grades that contained a parent-participation component. The longitudinal study, carried out by researchers at the University of North Carolina, examined the effects of preschool education combined with a home-school resource program for early elementary grades on the scholastic achievements of pupils at risk for academic failure (Ramey and Haskins 1981). The school-age phase of this study took place between 1977 and 1985. The experience gained from this phase of the study gave the pro-

ject's home-school teachers valuable insights into ways to work with and through parents to enhance students' achievement.

The Study

The subjects in the research were children from economically disadvantaged families identified on the basis of a high-risk index given to their mothers around the time of the children's birth (Ramey and Smith 1977). The index included such factors as age of mother, family income, and the length of the parents' schooling. All subject families had low incomes, and most were single-parent families headed by a young woman with less than a high school education. Children were assigned to treatment groups, whether preschool or school age, at random. The preschool treatment had no formal parent-involvement component.

As the study's children entered public kindergarten, the groups were redistributed, and half the preschool experimental group and half the control group were randomly assigned a home-school teacher to act as a liaison between the child's home and the classroom. The home-school teacher worked with the child, the parent, and the classroom teacher to bring about a smooth transition from preschool to primary education and to furnish a systematic way for high-risk parents to reinforce and enhance their child's early learning in public school. During the first three years of elementary school, the home-school teacher met regularly with the classroom teacher to determine which skills were being taught and which skills the pupil needed to practice, then designed individualized educational activities and presented these to the parents with instructions on how to use them with their children. Mathematics and reading were the two academic areas emphasized in these parent-child activities.

Preliminary findings indicate that this parent-involvement strategy, coupled with the early preschool intervention, did produce higher academic achievement for treated pupils compared to achievement levels attained by the control group. For mathematics specifically, at the end of three years in school, high-risk children who had preschool and school-age intervention attained a mean grade equivalent score of 2.94, or achievement at the fifty-first percentile, as compared to a mean grade quivalent of 2.43, or an average score at the thirty-third percentile, for the control group.

Suggestions for Involving Parents

The methods used in the home-school phase of this research project to elicit parents' involvement in their children's education can be adapted for use by regular classroom teachers. Some specific suggestions for involving parents in mathematics activities are outlined in the following:

1. Set up a simple system and introduce it to each parent individually.

Not every pupil will need extra practice in mathematics. The teacher should target the pupils who might benefit from supplemental activities and conact their parents individually. During a meeting or a telephone call, the process for working with a child at home can be fully explained. The teacher can describe the type of mathematics actvities to be sent home for the parent and child to work on together. The parents are told that directions for each activity will be supplied and that the parent can contact the teacher if any questions or problems arise.

Teachers might initially need to encourage parents to ask for explanations and even prompt them to do so by contacting the parents to ask about the activity. Teachers may even ask the parents to suggest ways to improve the activities. This request from the teacher for feedback could help to create a sense of teamwork between parents and the school and also serve to build parents' confidence.

2. Be certain that the parents are asked to work with a child at the child's ability level.

Classroom teachers should be thoroughly aware of a pupil's understanding of skills before sending any materials home. Parents should work with their child to practice skills for mastery and reinforcement rather than teach new skills. Parents, especially unsophisticated parents, may become easily frustrated if their child cannot comprehend the concept being worked on. All home activities should promote both parental success and pupils' self-confidence.

3. Clarify how mathematics skills are sequenced.

When presenting materials to parents, teachers need to emphasize the specific skill the pupil needs to master and why this mastery is an important step in the sequence of mathematics skills. Parents need to understand the importance of building on mastered skills. For example, they should know that a pupil practices combining groups of objects so that she or he can be successful in addition.

4. Give parents clear, *individual* instruction.

Parents' needs and abilities vary just as their children's do. Some parents require much more guidance than others when they begin to work with their children on mathematics activities. Even parents with a high level of skill in mathematics may be uncertain how to teach elementary mathematics to their own children and would, therefore, appreciate concise directions for the activities. Written explanations should accompany all mathematics activities sent home to give simple yet complete instructions on how to use each material (see tables 1 and 2**).**

Parents need to be told if pupils should use manipulatives and if finger counting is allowed. A pupil's lack of understanding can be pointed out to the parents by asking the parent to have the child perform common procedures, such as counting objects (one-to-one correspondence), finding a page in a book (sequencing), or counting backward (beginning subtraction). With specific examples, parents can more easily see their child's

Table 1

Directions for Home Activities for Beginning Combination of Numbers and Sequence of Numbers

I. Goal: Your child will match mathematics problems with dominoes with the same numbers.
    Materials: dominoes, mathematics addition cards
    1. Have your child match the dots on the dominoes with number-fact cards, for example,

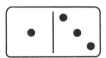

    2. When she can do this easily, time her on matching all the cards to dominoes. See if she can match them again, beating her time.
II. Goal: Your child will be able to identify the number that is one more or one less than a numeral.
    Materials: number cards 1–10
    1. Show your child one number card at a time. Have her tell you what number is *one more* than the number that is on the card.
    2. Repeat the activity, showing her a number and asking what number is *one less*.

Table 2

Directions for Home Activities of Place-Value and Subtraction-Fact Drill

I. Goal: Your child will be able to state the place value of each digit in a two-digit number (10's and 1's).

Materials: tens sticks, ones squares, number cards for 10–99

  1. Put out a number card, for example, 62. Have your child tell you how many tens and how many ones are in the numeral (6 sticks, 2 squares). Go through all the cards with your child; he should tell you the number and then put out the correct number of tens and ones.

  2. Make a number by putting out some sticks and squares, for example, two sticks plus two squares is twenty-two. Have your child tell you the number.

II. Goal: Your child will be able to subtract numbers quickly and corectly from ten.

Materials: A game board with incremental spaces leading to the finish line, markers, mathematics flash cards, counters

  1. Put the flash cards face down. Each player draws a card during his or her turn, answers the problem, and moves that many spaces. the first player to reach the end wins the game. (Your child may need to use counters when solving the problems.)

  2. Go through the cards with your child. After he is finished, have him count how many problems he solved correctly. Go throughthe cards again. Have your child try to solve more problems correctly the second time.

need for mathematics practice and may also think of other activities involving everyday routine that would reinforce the skills needed.

5. Supply the materials.

Having teachers make and distribute the materials may be time-consuming at first, but it is an important guarantee that some parental involvement in the mathematics activity will occur. Classroom teachers have commonly asked parents to make flash cards for mathematics drill. The providers of the experimental home-school program described here found, however, that even if the parent was so directed, the flash cards were rarely made at home. When the home-school teachers supplied the flash cards to the parents, along with specific and interesting ways to use the cards to drill mathematics facts with their children, parents generally followed through.

Reusable materials reduce the teacher's work load. Some of the materials can be sent out with a pupil on a two-week loan and then, if returned, used by another pupil on a two-week basis. Rewards may be needed to ensure that the materials are returned. Other materials can be throwaways, such as calendar pages to be cut up for sequencing of numbers or advertisement stamps to be used in one-to-one counting. Classroom teachers should not assume that parents have materials, even magazines, at home or that they are willing to use household materials for mathematics.

6. Furnish activities that are entertaining and take only a short time to complete.

Parents and pupils should be able to enjoy the mathematics activity so that they will view the time working together in a positive way. Parents are also more likely to follow through with activities that take less than ten minutes a night. (Parents in the experimental study reported working with their children on both mathematics and reading activities for an average of fifteen minutes each day.) Classroom teachers should emphasize that although very little time is needed to complete an activity each night, the activities should be used consistently, four to five nights a week. The hope is that the parent will set aside a specific time each day to make it easier to keep to a schedule. This frequency of presentation not only allows the pupil to master the skill more quickly and completely but makes parental involvement in mathematics a part of the daily routine.

7. Ask for feedback and give praise.

Parents can give the teacher information on the usefulness of the activity and the pupil's progress in the targeted mathematics skill. The reporting can be encouraged by attaching a form to the materials sent home asking the parent to send back any comments (see table 3). Telephone contacts or brief meetings with the parents to discuss mathematics activities may also be beneficial but are not always feasible.

Table 3

Parents' Form for Evaluation of Home Activities

Activity_____

Please rate this activitiy on the following scales after you and your child have worked with it.

1	2	3	4	5
Easy for my child				Very difficult
1	2	3	4	5
Child enjoyed activity				Child didn't like activity
1	2	3	4	5
Completed in 10 min. or less	15 min.	20 min,	25 min.	Took 30 min, or longer complete
1	2	3	4	5
Directions were easy to understand				Direction made no sense

Comments:

Parents appreciate acknowledgment of their efforts. If their children show progress in mathematics, this outcome will be reinforcing, but praise from the classroom teacher can also greatly enhance the parents' sense of esteem and give the impetus for continuing parental involvement. Even a simple note sent home to the parents will accomplish this goal, but a personal contact or telephone call may be the optimum method for complimenting parents on their efforts.

8. Use parental involvement judiciously.

Few parents could work enthusiastically with their children on school work every night for a sustained period. "Give me a break" will eventually be voiced by either parent or child, or both. Mathematics activities should be sent home at specific times during the year when the teacher identifies a skill with which the pupil needs structured practice. Giving several interesting games or activities to the parent at this point should be an incentive for parents and child to work on the skill systematically. Make the activity part of the homework routine for a specified amount of time, and then praise parents and child for their efforts.

Conclusion

These eight tenets of parental involvement have been addressed again and again throughout the years of the homeschool component of the research project. Having parents work with their children to reinforce mathematics skills has been shown to enhance achievement levels in that subject for early elementary school pupils. Even mathematically unsophisticated parents can become natural partners of teachers in the educational process if given materials to use and guidelines for how to use them effectively and if also made to feel that they are making an important contribution to the child's academic progress. From the experience gained in this study, it was clear that parents can and want to be involved in their child's education. The way the classroom teacher proceeds to obtain this involvement is an important factor in its success.

The insights shared here are experiential, based on a program in which an estimated 4000 mathematics activities were delivered to families for use by parents. Parents reported they enjoyed the experience and regretted that it did not continue past the third elementary school year. Teachers, similarly, often expressed regret that the same supplements were not available for some of the nonprogram pupils in their classroom. The methods described here could be adopted by classroom teachers. With a little extra planning, parents can be a ready resource.

References

Bodner-Johnson, Barbara. "The Family Environment and Achievement of Deaf Students: A Discriminant Analysis." *Exceptional Children* 52 (August 1986): 443–49.

Bronfenbrenner, Urie. "Is Early Intervention Effective?" In *Handbook of Evaluation Research*, edited by M. Guttentag and E. L. Struening, 2. Beverly Hills, Calif.: Sage Publications, 1975.

Epstein, Joyce L., and Henry J. Becker. "Teacher's Reported Practices of Parent Involvement: Problems and Possibilities." *Elementary School Journal* 83 (November 1982): 103–13.

Glass, Julia O. M. "An Evaluation of a Parental Involvement Program." Ph.D. diss., Georgia State University, 1977. *Dissertation Abstracts International* 38 (1978): 3839A.

Grimmet, Sadie, and Mae McCoy. "Effects of Parental Communication on Reading Performance of Third Grade Children." *Reading Teacher* 34 (December 1980): 303–8.

Hayes, Edward J., George K. Cunningham, and Joseph B. Robinson. "Counseling Focus: Are Parents Necessary?" *Elementary School Guidance and Counseling* 12 (October 1977): 8–14.

Kroth, Roger L., and Geraldine J. Scholl. *Getting Schools Involved with Parents.* Arlington, Va.: Council for Exceptional Children, 1978.

Ramey, Craig T., and Ron Haskins. "The Causes and Treatment of School Failure: Insights from the Carolina Abecedarian Project." In Psychosocial Influences and Retarded Performance: Strategies for Improving Social Competence, 2. Baltimore: University Park Press, 198 1.

Ramey, Craig T., and Barbara Smith. "Assessing the Intellectual Consequences of Early Intervention with High-Risk Infants." *American Journal of Mental Deficiency* 81 (November 1977): 318–24.

Teller, Henry E. "The Relationship of Parent Attitudes with Successful Integration of Hearing Impaired Children into Regular Classrooms." Ph.D. diss., University of Alabama, 1974. *Dissertation Abstracts International* 36 (1975) :821–22A.

Part 2
Family Participation in School Settings

A Fourth-Grade Family Math Night

Jane B. Hall and Rita P. Acri

September entry) Our fourth graders arrived this year full of excitement about mathematics. We hope that we can "dust ourselves off" and once again keep the subject alive and interesting for them. To develop mathematical power in all students, our district's goals are these:

- To help students attain solid mathematics skills

- To connect mathematics to students' everyday lives

- To stress thinking skills in problem solving

- To help students discover the fun of doing mathematics, reinforcing their positive attitudes

We would also like to get parents involved because we need their help to make this a great year. I will have to think more about it.

(January entry) Mathematics class is going smoothly now, but the fourth-grade teachers all feel that some of the children's enthusiasm is slipping. We have not really involved the parents yet, but we have an idea for that—we will have a family night and use the "math power" theme.

Maybe some self-directed-learning stations for students and their parents would work. We could select different stations to show the variety of things

Jane Hall teaches fourth grade in the East Pennsboro Area School District, Enola, PA 17025. She uses hands-on activities and real-life problem-solving situations when teaching mathematics. Rita Acri is the district's mathematics department chair for grades K–12. She is working to implement NCTM's standards in the district.

we do in mathematics that connect to the district's goals. Some of the details will include prizes to be obtained, MATH POWER buttons to be made, brochures to be typed, photos to be taken, and refreshments to be ordered. We will have to reserve the cafeteria and invite the press. This activity will take several weeks of preparation, but it sounds like it will be worth the effort.

(February entry) All is ready! We have the cafeteria reserved from 7:00 p.m. to 8:30 p.m. next Thursday. Forty-five (out of 96) fourth graders have signed up to come with at least one parent. A few siblings may also attend, but we have tried to encourage fourth graders and parents only.

I will go over the plans one final time in my mind. On arriving, each family will stop at the registration table. All fourth graders will get a MATH POWER button, a door-prize entry form, and a fast-food coupon. Parents will get a printed program listing the activity stations and containing various announcements and directions. They will also receive a survey sheet to be completed later, to let us know what they thought of the evening.

At 8:00 p.m. I will remind everyone to write their estimate for the Bestimator Estimator contest, and then at 8:10 p.m. we will start giving out prizes. Three lucky individuals will take home a container of candy. Enough calculators and coupons for fast food, roller skating, and miniature golf are available so that every student wins a door prize. It is gratifying that all the businesses we contacted donated prizes.

31

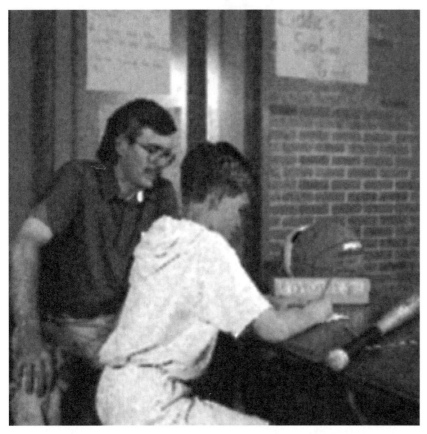

Students worked as equals with their parents.

(March entry) We were so busy at Family Math Night that I was too tired to jot down notes about the stations. I will do it now! The pictures have been developed so I can include them also.

1. The Price Is Right: We put different sizes of some common grocery items on a table, being sure that the price and size were visible on each. The students and their parents then found the unit price of each item and determined the best buy. They discovered that "giant economy size" is not always a bargain.

2. Calculator Corner: We found some challenging activities in *How to Develop Problem Solving Using a Calculator*. Parent and child discussed how to use the calculator efficiently to solve the problem. This station presented an opportunity for students to show their parents the problem-solving strategies that they had learned in the classroom.

3. Chinese Tangrams: We made copies, on fluorescent paper, of the original tangram square for participants to cut out. We laminated six patterns taken from *Tangrams, 330 Puzzles* by Ronald Read (1965). Some of the students demonstrated better spatial sense than their parents in placing the seven tangram pieces onto each shape. Adults and students found this activity to be especially challenging and fun!

4. Sporting Goods Shop: The physical education teacher loaned us some sports equipment, and we put large price tags on them. Both students and parents mentally estimated the total cost then found the exact answer using a calculator. This activity went well, particularly when the students wrote "pretend" checks for the purchase.

5. Off to the Races: This station involved a clever way to show probability and statistics. At the table

were four pictures of cars, each one with fifteen circles on it. The cars were labeled 0, 1, 2, and 3, respectively.

Two adults and two students played, each choosing a car for the race. They flipped three coins in the air simultaneously, and the resulting number of heads determined which race car would have a circle covered by a marker. The game continued until one car won by having all its circles covered. We charted the winners, which showed that only cars 1 and 2 would win.

I carried this game over into my classroom the next day. In groups the children were able to explore the mathematics behind the result:

Possible Outcomes	Winner
H, H, H	"3" car
H, H, T	"2" car
H, T, T	"1" car
H, T, H	"2" car
T, T, T	"0" car
T, T, H	"1" car
T, H, H	"2" car
T, H, T	"1" car

They found that cars 1 and 2 had a three times greater chance of winning than cars 0 and 3. They enjoyed this game. In the future we will plan to try other probability activities.

6. Bestimator Estimator: We had pre-counted the candy and filled three containers of different shapes, each with about the same volume of one quart. Each person made one estimate of the number of candies in each container. At the end of the evening, the person with the closest estimate, plus or minus, won the container full of candy. This activity proved to be quite popular with children and adults.

7. Entertain the Brain: We made laminated copies of brainteasers and logic problems with answers on the reverse side of the paper. Some of these puzzlers came from *Welcome Quik-Wits: Critical Thinking and*

Problem Solving, Grade 4 (Hayes and Sebastian 1989). It was rewarding to see the parents try to solve the problems with algebra while their children succeeded in solving them with fourth-grade arithmetic. This activity is a "keeper" for next year.

8. Twenty-Four: We put out a game to show that we have not forgotten basic arithmetic and that even computation can be challenging and meaningful if it involves a strategy. Twenty-Four, a game from Suntex International, was a good choice. The object was to be the first player to make 24 with all four numbers on a card by adding, subtracting, multiplying, or dividing. The cards are coded for three levels of difficulty. Students were surprised at their parents' computing abilities, and all enjoyed this game.

Enough notes for one night!

(April entry) I cannot believe that it has been four weeks since our Family Math Night. It sure seemed to perk up the fourth graders and their "mid-year doldrums." What I remember most vividly was the students' ability to work as equals with their parents on the problems. Some parent-child teams hurried through all the stations, of course, but others spent almost the entire night on one problem. The variety of approaches were typical of those that I see in my classroom.

The principal helped set up and take down the work stations, and even the custodial staff helped out after the event was over. Many of the parents said how much they enjoyed the evening, and that feedback alone was worth the effort.

Some teams spent the entire night on one problem.

Family Math Night is a must for next year! Now that the word has spread to the third graders, they will be looking forward to it. We should not be tempted to do it too early, though—we should hold off until the year has lost momentum and "midwinter blues" have set in. We can save the photographs and use them on a poster next year, before the Second Annual Fourth-Grade Family Math Night, to let students know what to expect and to encourage them to attend.

Bibliography

Bayliffe, Janie, Raymond Brie, and Beverly Oliver. "Teaching Mathematics with Technology: Family Math Enhanced through Technology." *Arithmetic Teacher* 41 (November 1993): 172–75.

Hayes, Joy, and Marion M. Sebastian. *Welcome Quik-Wits: Critical Thinking, Problem Solving, Gr. 4.* Minneapolis: Judy/Instructo, 1989.

Jacobs, Jean W. "Purr-r-r-fectly Wild about Mathematics." *Arithmetic Teacher* 37 (December 1989): 4–5.

Morris, Janet. *How to Develop Problem Solving Using a Calculator.* Reston, Va.: National Council of Teachers of Mathematics, 1981.

National Council of Teachers of Mathematics. *Curriculum and Evaluation Standards for School Mathematics.* Reston, Va.: The Council, 1989.

National PTA. *Math Matters: Kids Are Counting on You.* Chicago: Author, 1989.

Peterson, Winnie. "Principles for Principals." *Arithmetic Teacher* 36 (March 1989): 24.

Read, Ronald C. *Tangrams, 330 Puzzles.* New York: Dover Publications, 1965.

Stenmark, Jean Kerr, Virginia Thompson, and Ruth Cossey. *Family Math.* Berkeley, Calif.: University of California Regents, 1986.

Math Is FUNctional!
A Math Fair for Kids

Barbara J. Reys and Deanna G. Wasman

How do you show students that mathematics can be recreational as well as practical? How do you give preservice teachers authentic opportunities to design and facilitate mathematics activities to motivate students? How do you involve parents in looking at mathematics from a nontraditional viewpoint? We found a way to address each of these important goals by sponsoring a Saturday-morning Math Fair for Kids using NCTM's promotional theme "Math Is FUNctional" (with the emphasis on FUN).

The UM²TO (University of Missouri Mathematics Teachers Organization) is an affiliated group of NCTM whose members are college students planning and preparing for a career in teaching mathematics, K–12. Its members meet monthly in an informal setting to interact, share experiences, and learn ways to maximize their preparation for teaching. As a service project, the organization sponsored a mathematics fair for fifth graders. In part, the fair was prompted by a desire to serve the community. It offered the opportunity to show the "fun" side of mathematics to students as well as parents. It also encouraged future teachers to research and become familiar with a range of mathematics games, puzzles, and experiments. Fifth grade was chosen as the target audience for the fair because it is the final year of elementary school in the local school district. Targeting a limited, specific audience facilitated advertising the fair and furnished a guide to gauge the appropriateness of the mathematics activities included in the fair booths.

The fair was held on a Saturday morning in late winter before the preservice teachers began a formal student-teaching experience. Judging by the comments of the

Barbara Reys, cibr@showme.missouri.edu, is a professor of mathematics education at the University of Missouri, Columbia, MO 65211. Her interests include teacher preparation and number sense. Deanna Wasman is a doctoral student in mathematics education at the University of Missouri. She is teaching calculus at Hickman High School, Columbia, MO 65201.

students and their parents and by the interactions among booth organizers and students, the fair was a huge success. Here we summarize how the fair was developed and conducted, including a brief description of some of the activities at the fair and some suggestions for making such a fair a success. We hope that this information might motivate other groups, such as college-student organizations, PTAs, and teachers, to develop and offer a fair.

Planning and Organization

The fair was organized as a series of booths, each with a different mathematical theme. Each booth was developed and run by a team of two to three college students. In addition to staffing the booth on the day of the fair, they gathered necessary materials and game boards and prepared handouts to be used for the activity of the booth. They also decorated their booth to coordinate with the activity and prepared posters highlighting or announcing their booth. For example, the Math Magic booth organizers wore "swami" outfits and decorated their booth to coincide with a mystery theme. Finally, each team of booth organizers prepared a one-page handout describing their activity, game, or puzzle so that students would have something to take home to continue their exploration. Twenty mathematics-theme booths were formed by eight-foot tables decorated with a mathematical or fair theme; some of the booth themes are described in the next section.

The registration procedure for the fair included getting a name tag, a schedule of booths, and a bag donated by a local bookstore for storing handouts and prizes. We printed the list of booth names on cardstock and tied string around it so students could wear the "fair schedule" around their necks and thus free their hands to explore. Students were allowed to move from booth to booth in any order as their interest dictated. They could spend as much time at a booth

as they wished. Parents were given the option to stay with their child, roam the fair on their own, or come back to pick up their child at a later time. About two-thirds of the parents chose to stay for the fair with their children.

The fair schedule included an area where booth organizers could place a stamp to indicate that the student had participated in their booth activity. When a student had accumulated four stamps, he or she was eligible to go to the prize booth to draw from the prize jar, which contained slips of paper naming various prizes. The prizes were mathematics-related items that were either donated by a local business or purchased by UM²TO. The prizes included "I love math" stickers and buttons, "5th graders are great" pencils, and coupons for food at local fast-food restaurants. In addition, UM²TO had ten "Math Is FUNctional" T-shirts printed and available as prizes.

Three rooms at the fair were set aside for other activities: one for showing the mathematics films *The Weird Number* and *Mathematical Peep Show;* another for exploration of the computer programs The Geometer's Sketchpad, Kaleid-a-Tile, and Tesselmania; and the third for building three-dimensional models with such manipulatives as polydrons and multilink cubes. The show times for the videos were posted, and students and parents were encouraged to come and go as they liked. A game area for students featured a collection of classic, commercially available games and puzzles, such as SomaCube; Topspin; Back-Spin; Conway's Cube; Frustration; Gordian Knot; and Mancala, an African stone game.

Booths

A variety of booths appealed to different interests, including games involving numbers and computation, logic puzzles, geometry and spatial-visualization exploration, and probability and statistics activities. This section summarizes thirteen of the twenty booths. We found Family Math

(Stenmark, Thompson, and Cossey 1986) and *The Good Time Math Event Book* (Burns 1977) to be excellent sources of ideas for fair booths.

Number games

Fabulous 15. In this two-player game, each player takes turns choosing a number from 1 to 9 and placing the number on a three-by-three grid. The goal is to place in a row three numbers whose sum is fifteen before the other player does. The numbers can be used only once. The traditional magic square provides a successful strategy for winning the game.

The Game of 99. Two to five players can join in this card game to practice mental computation. Five regular playing cards are dealt to each player. The remaining cards are stacked facedown in the center. Players take turns laying a card down from their hands and then drawing another card from the deck. When a player lays a card down, he or she must add the value of the card to the running total of the discard pile. Play continues in this manner until one player is forced to go over ninety-nine, which means that he or she is out of the game. Special-value cards include 4: reverse order of play, K: sum immediately goes to ninety-nine, 7: skip my turn, 10: subtract ten, A: add one, and all other face cards: add ten.

The Factor Game. The game board consists of the numbers 1–30 on a laminated poster board. Two players take turns choosing a number. After choosing a number, the player circles it. Then the opponent circles all factors of this number. The play continues until no numbers remain with uncircled factors. After the numbers that each player circled are added, the player with the greater total wins.

Large-Number Planet. An eight-foot-high dodecahedron attracted the attention of many students. The dodecahedron represented the sun. On the basis of this model, students were asked to choose balls of different sizes to represent other planets and to locate the planets' relative positions along the hallway.

Estimation. A series of estimation contests were presented at this booth each half-hour. Students participated in each contest by making an estimate, which was recorded on paper and dropped into a jar for later review. The contests included the following estimations: How many paper clips would be needed to reach from floor to ceiling? How many pretzels are in the jar? How many people are attending the fair? In a nationwide sample, what percent of fifth graders indicated that mathematics is their favorite subject?

Logic games and puzzles

Tower of Hanoi. This ancient puzzle consists of three pegs and seven discs of different sizes. The object is to shift all the discs from the center peg to one of the outside pegs. You may move only one disc at a time and may not place a larger disc on a smaller disc. How many moves are required?

Math Magic. The two leaders of this booth dressed up like swamis to "read the minds" of students. Six binary-number cards were used (see fig. 1). The swamis asked the students to think of a number between one and sixty-three. Then, after asking whether that number appeared on card 1, card 2, card 3, and so on, they announced the number that the student had chosen. The student was then asked whether he or she could figure out the "trick."

Pico, Fermi, Bagels. The students are encouraged to use deductive thinking to guess a three-digit number. The clues are offered in the way of "Pico," "Fermi," or "Bagel." "Pico" indicates to the student the number of digits that are correct but in the wrong place. "Fermi" indicates the number of digits that are correct and in the right place. "Bagel" indicates the number of digits that are incorrect. The student continues guessing and using the clues until he or she deduces the mystery number.

Three-Bean Salad. The students are given a tray with red beans, lima beans, and black-eyed peas in three different compartments. They choose from among eight different "salads" that they could make (see fig. 2). One salad recipe calls for an equal number of red beans and black-eyed peas, five more lima beans than red beans, and no more than twenty beans. The booth organizers rewarded successful salad mixtures with various small prizes, such as stickers.

Geometry and spatial visualization

Get a TANgram by the Sea. With Caribbean music playing to create atmosphere, the students used tangrams to make various shapes and pictures. They were also invited to make their own sets of tangrams using craft foam pads.

Rectangular Tetris. This activity starts with rolling two number cubes (see fig. 3). The two numbers rolled represent the dimensions of a rectangle. After rolling the cubes, the student shades the rectangle on a nine-by-seventeen grid. The rectangles cannot overlap. When a player cannot fit a rectangle on the grid, he or she is finished. A score is calculated by counting the number of unshaded squares in the original nine-by-eighteen rectangle. The booth organizers posted scores on a chart and invited students to go for a lower, or better, score.

Probability and statistics

What's in a Bag of M&M's? Miniature bags of M&M's were used to investigate such ideas as histograms, frequency, probability, and ratios. After opening a bag of M&M's, the student placed the orange M&M's in a column on a sheet of graph paper. Repeating this arrangement for each of the colors, students created their own histograms and recorded the results. Students were asked whether this distribution would be the same for another bag of M&M's. The results of each individual bag were compiled on a large wall-mounted chart. As more students did the activity, the data set grew, and students continued to compare their graph with the larger chart.

Rock, Paper, Scissors. Three people played this game by showing, after a count to three, an open hand for paper, a "V" with two fingers for scissors, or a fist for rock. Tallies were kept for the following categories: all three players match, only two match, and no matches. After the data were

---

I Can Read Your Mind!		
1 3 5 7	2 3 6 7	4 5 6 7
9 11 13 15	10 11 14 15	12 13 14 15
17 19 21 23	18 19 22 23	20 21 22 23
25 27 29 31	26 27 30 31	28 29 30 31
33 35 37 39	34 35 38 39	36 37 38 39
41 43 45 47	42 43 46 47	44 45 46 47
49 51 53 55	50 51 54 55	52 53 54 55
57 59 61 63	58 59 62 63	60 61 62 63
8 9 10 11	16 17 18 19	32 33 34 35
12 13 14 15	20 21 22 23	36 37 38 39
24 25 26 27	24 25 26 27	40 41 42 43
28 29 30 31	28 29 30 31	44 45 46 47
40 41 42 43	48 49 50 51	48 49 50 51
44 45 46 47	52 53 54 55	52 53 54 55
56 57 58 59	56 57 58 59	56 57 58 59
60 61 62 63	60 61 62 63	60 61 62 63

Instructions:
1. Make six cards with numbers on them exactly as shown above.
2. Ask a friend to think of a whole number between 1 and 63.
3. Ask your friend if the number is on the first card. Then ask if the number is on the second card. Then ask if the number is on the third card, the fourth card, the fifth card, and the sixth card.
4. You can know what number your friend is thinking of just from the answers to these six questions. Can you figure out how?

Fig. 1. Math Magic game cards

Three-Bean Salad
All three types of beans go into each salad:
red beans, lima beans, and black-eyed peas.

1

This salad contains 2 lima beans; twice as many red beans as lima beans; 10 beans in all.

2

This salad contains 4 red beans; 1/2 as many black-eyed peas as red beans; 10 beans in all.

3

Lima beans make up 1/2 of this salad: The salad has exactly 2 red beans. The number of lima beans is double the number of red beans.

4

This salad contains the same number of red beans as lima beans; 3 more black-eyed peas than red beans; a total of 18 beans.

5

This salad contains 12 beans. One-half of the beans are red. Lima beans make up 1/4 of the salad.

6

This salad contains at least 12 beans. It has one more lima bean than red beans. It has one more red bean than black-eyed peas.

7

This salad contains 3 times as many red beans as black-eyed peas; one more lima bean than red beans; 8 beans in all.

8

This salad contains an equal number of red beans and black-eyed peas; 5 more lima beans than red beans; no more than 20 beans.

Fig. 2. Three-Bean-Salad activity card

collected for several trials, students were asked to explore, with the assistance of booth organizers, the probability of each outcome.

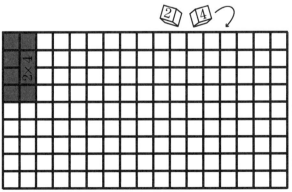

Fig. 3. Rectangular Tetris activity

Tips for Developing a Mathematics Fair

Here are some questions and suggestions for those who are considering doing a mathematics fair. They are based on our one-time experience. For other ideas, see the bibliography for a list of articles related to mathematics fairs.

Offer prizes for the best booths. One goal of the mathematics fair was to offer a good learning experience for preservice teachers who served as booth developers and facilitators. They worked hard on the task of developing booths. We asked one group of six students who had participated in the fair to vote on their favorite booths. These votes were counted, and prizes of $10 NCTM gift certificates were awarded to the organizers of the three best booths. The most popular booths at our fair were the solar system, Pico-Fermi-Bagels, and What's in a Bag of M&M's?

Offer prizes for the students. Once students experienced four booths and received four stamps on their schedule cards, they could draw for a prize. The intent was to distribute a number of prizes equitably. The possibility of a prize stimulated a number of students to "go back for more." Several parents indicated they had planned to leave before the end of the fair but that their students insisted on staying "to do more booths," both because they enjoyed them and because they wanted to get another prize.

Develop a tracking system to document what the students are doing. The "booth schedule" listed the names, locations, and brief descriptions of the various booths. It provided a place for individual booth organizers to document participation by placing a stamp in a square. This system allowed us to distribute prizes fairly and helped advertise various booths to students.

Develop and post lots of signs directing students to various fair locations. Signs were used for practical purposes of directing students to various locations and also for purposes of entertainment and advertisement. For example, a series of signs, including mathematics riddles, comics, and optical illusions, was posted near the refreshment area and in the hallways to provide yet another opportunity to enjoy mathematics. Some booth organizers developed and posted signs to attract students to their booths.

Include video and computer exploration. The video, computer, and model-building rooms offered a place for "overflow" crowds; more students could work in these rooms at a time than could work at any one booth.

Do not forget refreshments. Keeping students physically nourished as well as mentally nourished is an important part of the details in putting on a fair. Local fast-food restaurants and grocery stores were gracious in donating cookies and juice for this purpose.

Choose a target audience. We found it helpful to identify a specific target audience, fifth grade, for the fair. Although other younger and older students found their way into the fair, the booths were developed to involve mathematics appropriate for about fifth grade.

Prepare handouts for parents and students. Each pair of booth organizers prepared a one- or two-page handout describing their game, puzzle, or activity. This aspect gave college students an authentic opportunity to describe an activity in writing and generated something tangible for students and parents to take home to continue the activity.

Invite and involve area mathematics-club students. If you need additional help, involve area mathematics-club students (elementary, junior high, or senior high) or high school teacher-cadet members to help organize a booth or to staff the computer and video rooms.

Offer options and information for parents. Many parents stayed for the fair, either to participate as a partner with their child or to roam the fair on their own. A special series of NCTM brochures was made available to parents. We plan to include the showing of a special video for parents in the next fair.

What is a good ratio of booths to students? We suggest a ratio of about one booth for every six to eight students who attend the fair. This ratio will spread the students out and ensure that students do not need to wait in line for any length of time.

What is a good ratio of adults to students? At least two adults are needed to staff each booth. In addition, adults are needed to register the stu-

dents and to staff the prize, refreshment, computer, video, and model-building rooms. In general, one adult is needed for every four to five students.

How do you advertise the fair? We developed a flyer announcing the purpose, audience, time, and location of the fair and distributed one set of flyers to each fifth-grade teacher in the local school district. In addition, a public-service announcement on the local AM-radio station announced the activity the week before the fair.

What about preregistration? The announcement flyer included a pre-registration form. Students were asked to share the flyer with their parents and return the registration information three weeks before the fair. This form allowed us to gauge the number of participants. In addition, some students responded to the public-service announcement and so did not preregister.

What is the cost? The total cost of the fair was about $500. The bulk of the cost was for printing flyers; supplying prizes; and getting such supplies as balloons, helium, and poster board. Some prizes were donated, thus reducing the cost of the fair. The UM²TO was awarded a grant of $200 by the University Student Association. If we had anticipated the need for additional resources, we would likely have sought support from the NCTM's affiliated-group grant fund.

Summary

About 120 people participated in the first annual UM²TO Math Fair for Kids, including students, parents, preservice teachers, and university faculty. After the fair, we received a number of calls from parents thanking us for the opportunity that the fair offered their children. Several even asked if it would be a "monthly" event!

As a follow-up, we plan to send out a newsletter to the students who participated in the fair, alerting them to other mathematics-oriented opportunities in the area—contests, science

fairs, Internet puzzle pages, and the like.

Since this was our first experience doing a fair, we were a bit conservative on advertising, wanting to make sure that we could do it well on a small scale before involving a larger group of students. Now that we have some sense of the amount of work involved as well as how to organize a fair, we plan to use the information as we develop the next annual fair. We have no doubt in our minds that it is a worthwhile activity for all involved.

Bibliography

Burns, Marilyn. *The Good Time Math Event Book.* Mountain View, Calif.: Creative Publications, 1977.

Dehan, Harriet. "A Mathematical Magic Show." *Mathematics Teacher* 83 (October 1990): 515–23.

Glassman, Jerrold. "Add School Spice: Whip Up Enthusiasm with a Math Fair." *Executive Educator* 6 (January 1984): 15–26.

Hall, Jane, and Rita Acri. "A Fourth-Grade Family Math Night." *Teaching Children Mathematics* 2 (September 1995): 8–10.

McCarty, Diane. "Fairs with a Flair." *Teaching K–8* (January 1996): 56–58.

O'Dowd, Kathy, and Marianne Franz. "Immersed in Math." *Instructor* 100 (April 1991): 30, 32, 34–35.

Stenmark, Jean, Virginia Thompson, and Ruth Cossey. *Family Math.* Berkeley, Calif.: Lawrence Hall of Science, University of California, 1986.

WHERE ALL ARE WINNERS:
A MATHEMATICS OLYMPICS
FOR PARENTS, STUDENTS, AND TEACHERS

Mary T. Koes and Joy Faini Saab

Welcoming parents to the school environment to participate in a fun-filled mathematics-olympics learning activity promotes positive attitudes toward the school. Such participation instills a sense of pride in the educational achievements of the school, which translates into caring that each child is successful. Programs that involve parents from the planning through the implementation stage also foster a strong sense of mutual trust between homes and schools.

Involving all parties in mathematics activities can help facilitate the implementation of the National Council of Teachers of Mathematics's (NCTM) goals in school classrooms (Crosswhite, Dossey, and Frye 1989). A mathematics-olympics event can make several powerful statements that support the NCTM's *Curriculum and Evaluation Standards for School Mathematics* (1989):

1. People from all walks of life enjoy mathematics and are willing to take time out from busy schedules to share that enjoyment.

2. Mathematics is nonthreatening and fun.

3. A student, as an individual or as a member of a group, can have many successful and varied types of experiences with mathematics in a relatively short period of time.

Essential to a successful mathematics olympics is the support of the school principal and staff. Steps toward this goal include obtaining the principal's and teachers' approvals. During the preplanning stage, plans for the fifth-grade mathematics

Mary Koes teaches fifth grade at Saint Mary's School, Potsdam, NY 13676. She is interested in integrating subjects across the curriculum, promoting hands -on mathematics, and providing problem-solving activities as well as encouraging family involvement. Joy Saab teaches at West Virginia University, Morgantown, WV 26505-6122. She is interested in process-oriented, activity-based teaching methods incorporating the arts in education.

olympics were presented at a general Parent-Teacher Association meeting where participants approved funds for instructional mathematics games and manipulatives. These materials would ultimately become part of the school's mathematics laboratory collection and be available to all teachers.

Determining whether particular mathematics concepts need reinforcement in a gamelike setting was important. One teacher recommended that we include Battleship because students needed more experience with coordinate geometry. Another teacher suggested tangrams, a geometric manipulative, to increase the children's understanding of relationships among simple geometric figures. Both teachers concurred that a hands-on approach would work best for a mock-olympic setting, and they assisted in selecting manipulatives that would be of value to the school for a wide variety of lessons and ages.

Parent-volunteer committee chairs were invited to participate in the mathematics olympics as game leaders with the anticipation that they would find the activity worthwhile and help sponsor it in the future. Those leaders helped form the volunteer crew of parents, teachers, and a graduate student.

The six activities selected and the rationale for the selection of each were as follows:

1. Battleship (Milton Bradley) helps to improve the students' understanding of coordinate geometry and promotes strategic planning and logical thinking.

2. Tangram exercises, designed by one of the fifth-grade teachers, provide practice in solving puzzles and reinforcing geometric terms. The exercises also emphasize spatial reasoning.

3. Juggle (Del Regato 1980) requires the use of transformation geometry (rotations, flips, slides), spatial reasoning, metric measurement, and estimation.

4. "Fraction blackjack" (Bennett and Davidson 1973), an adaptation of a popular card game, focuses on the addition of fractions and improves mental-arithmetic and estimation skills.

5. Kalah (Brill 1974), an ancient count-and-capture game that originated in Africa, promotes logical strategies and patterns of thinking. The parent volunteer briefly explains the history of this fascinating game and demonstrates a round of play.

6. "Wheel of numbers," adapted from a popular television program, involves mental mathematics and estimation over varying skill levels.

With school approval and events planned, the parent director met with each game leader several days prior to the olympics to explain the philosophy of the event and to teach the game that the volunteer would be supervising (see fig. 1). A copy of the game was left with the volunteer so that he or she could practice before the event.

A poster-board invitation, incorporating the international Olympic Games logo, was extended to two fifth-grade classes. These invitations were posted in the classroom two weeks prior to the scheduled mathematics-olympics day. The fifth-grade teachers were asked to identify six

| Kalah games |
| Juggle games |
| Battleship |
| "Wheel of numbers" game |
| Pentominoes |
| Tangrams |
| Fraction playing cards |
| Fraction bars |
| Flat, silver-foil-covered peppermint candies |
| Star bookmarks |
| Pencils and paper |
| Small chalkboards and chalk |
| Timer |
| Name tags |

Fig. 1. List of materials for mathematics olympics

groups of students for each class. Each group was composed of four students of varying abilities. A parent volunteer prepared name tags for all participants.

Mathematics-Olympics Procedure

These procedures helped the games run smoothly.

1. One hour prior to the arrival of one class of students, desks were arranged in six groups of four around the perimeter of the room. A colored banner that identified the game area was placed in the center of each cluster of desks.

2. Volunteers arrived early and were given manila envelopes containing four flat, silver-foil-wrapped peppermint candies ("silver medals") and four star bookmarks to be given as small prizes to each student at the completion of all games. Name tags for each student and game leader were placed at each table.

3. Volunteers prepared their game areas.

4. Volunteers were asked to note high scores, if appropriate, but not to announce them publicly. This information would let future players know the previous high scores to challenge.

5. Students were welcomed and directed to their predetermined game centers. They were told that this olympics event was similar to the real Olympic Games in that they, the mathletes, had been in training for many years, both at school and at home. Unlike in the Olympic Games, no winner would be proclaimed, as the participants were already winners. Their challenge for the morning was simply to be good sports and have fun. Their endeavors would be rewarded with two small prizes, plus an assortment of new games for their mathematics laboratory.

6. The game leaders were introduced by the parent coordinator.

7. The teams were asked to move from one event to the next every fifteen minutes. The games continued for one hour and thirty minutes. Each student, either individually or as a team member, participated in six games during the course of the olympics. At the end of this period, game leaders for whom it was appropriate announced the highest scores achieved at their events, without referring to students' names.

8. The door prize, a jar of candy, was awarded to the student who most closely estimated the number of candies in that jar.

9. Game leaders collected name tags and presented silver "medals" and bookmarks to each student at his or her table.

10. At the end of the meet, students and game leaders completed evaluation forms designed to assess their enjoyment of the mathematics olympics and to solicit their ideas for improvement.

Results and Implications

All adult leaders indicated that they thoroughly enjoyed their mathematics-olympics experience and would be delighted to serve in that capacity again. Some leaders recommended extending the game periods from fifteen to twenty minutes each. The volunteers especially enjoyed observing the activities and helping the students develop game strategies. This indication of support could develop and grow through the Parent-Teacher Association as more parents have a chance to be involved in additional mathematics-olympics events. These types of events, along with class newsletters and workshops for parents, help parents to understand better the effectiveness of manipulative mathematics activities. The parents reflected positive reactions as they personally experienced the olympics events.

The value of such games as Pentominoes and kalah is that players have no readily available procedures for finding solutions, so the student can explore a wide variety of possibilities and feel good about original approaches to the games. In general, students seemed to have the greatest difficulty developing strategies to solve mental-arithmetic and estimation problems during the "wheel of numbers" game. Research suggests that the focus of school mathematics is often on the formal manipulation of symbols, discouraging students from using their intuition (Resnick 1989). The students' lack of comfort and apparent inexperience with approximating answers, in particular, point to the value of incorporating these types of activities in the daily mathematics lesson as recommended in NCTM's *Curriculum and Evaluation Standards for School Mathematics* (1989).

For most of these students, this event was their first experience with a mathematics olympics. The local school district sponsors an annual mathematics field day, but only the two top mathematics students from each class are invited to attend. The exuberant manner of each group as they proceeded from one event to the next was evidence of their total involvement with, motivation by, and enjoyment of instructional mathematics games.

For the next mathematics-olympics event, we plan to include more grade levels. Once the fifth-grade students, parents, and teachers started discussing this event, interest was generated throughout the school. With this first experience, it is now clear that planning and implementing a mathematics olympics as an annual event would be beneficial to all parents, teachers, and students involved.

We concur with Secada (1989) that schools must make available a broad range of opportunities for parental involvement because parents are a resource too precious to ignore. Our experience confirms that a mathematics olympics is a worthwhile educational opportunity for students and parents, one worthy of administrative and community support.

Bibliography

Bennett, Albert, and Patricia Davidson. *Fraction Bars: A Step by Step Workbook.* Fort Collins, Colo.: Scott Resources, 1973.

Brill, Randall L. "A Project for the Low-Budget Mathematics Laboratory: The Game of Kalah." *Arithmetic Teacher* 21 (February 1974): 659–61.

Crosswhite, F. Joe, John A. Dossey, and Shirley M. Frye. "National Council of Teachers of Mathematics: NCTM Standards for School Mathematics: Visions for Implementation." *Arithmetic Teacher* 37 (November 1989): 55–60.

Del Regato, John C. "Juggle." Indianapolis, Ind.: Pentathlon Institute, 1980.

Hollingsworth, Caroline. "Maximizing Implementation of Manipulatives." *Arithmetic Teacher* 37 (May 1990): 27.

Milton Bradley Co. "Battleship." Longmeadow, Mass.: Milton Bradley Co. Board game.

National Council of Teachers of Mathematics. *Curriculum and Evaluation Standards for School Mathematics.* Reston, Va.: The Council, 1989.

Resnick, Lauren B. "Developing Mathematical Knowledge." *American Psychologist* 44 (February 1989): 162–69.

Reys, Barbara, and Robert E. Reys. "Implementing the *Standards:* Estimation—Direction from the *Standards*." *Arithmetic Teacher* 37 (March 1990): 22–25.

Secada, Walter G. "Parental Involvement in a Time of Changing Demographics." *Arithmetic Teacher* 37 (December 1989): 33–35.

Resource Booklet

"Helping Your Child Learn Math", a forty-page booklet, features dozens of activities parents can use to help children have fun learning geometry, algebra, measurement, statistics, probability, and other mathematical concepts. These activities relate to everyday life and complement lessons that children learn in school. The materials used in the activities are easy to find and can easily be done in the home or car.

Other resources in the booklet include these:

- Mathematics-related Web sites with links for parents andchildren
- Mathematics computer software Web sites
- Mathematics books for parents and children

The booklet is available at the following Web site:
www.ed.gov/pubs/parents/Math/

Books + Manipulatives + Families = A Mathematics Lending Library

Diane McCarty

What do *Alexander, Who Used to Be Rich Last Sunday* (Viorst 1978), *Theodoric's Rainbow* (Kramer 1995), and *Grandfather Tang's Story* (Tompert 1990) have in common? They are all newly acquired books in the Price Laboratory Elementary Mathematics Lending Library—Connecting Home that was inaugurated in fall 1997. This project has been a long-term endeavor that began in spring 1996. At that time I received a $5000 grant to develop a lending library to support and extend the elementary mathematics curriculum. More specifically, the purpose of the library was to furnish another avenue for parents and students to read good literature together at home and to explore various mathematical concepts and skills at the same time.

The project, although still in its formative stage, is already showing a great deal of promise in meeting the basic objectives set forth in the original grant: (1) to implement the NCTM's connections standard (NCTM 1989); (2) to enhance parental involvement in mathematics learning; (3) to

Diane McCarty, diane.mccarty@uni.edu, is a fourth-grade teacher at Malcolm Price Laboratory School and an instructor at the University of Northern Iowa, Cedar Falls, IA 50613. Throughout her twenty years of teaching at every grade level, she has promoted the enjoyment of learning as a lifelong adventure.

Edited by Jacquelin Smith, 715 Maucker Road, Cedar Falls, IA 50613.

encourage active, hands-on approaches to mathematics in the home; and (4) to support curriculum integration. This article describes the process involved in the development of this whole-school project.

Grounded in Research

From the outset it was important that this project be firmly rooted in educational research. It needed to have a strong basis to gain the support not only of the elementary school staff but also of the parents served by our school. In addition, the project needed a solid base from which to continue to grow and improve. In undertaking the initial research, I encountered a great deal of support not only for the concept of the lending library itself but also for the underlying principles of learning involved.

With the advent of the *Curriculum and Evaluation Standards for School Mathematics* (NCTM 1989), a small revolution began in the way teachers were teaching mathematics. Many of the traditional methods, which greatly emphasized algorithms and memorization, were being replaced with an emphasis on understanding mathematics and being able to communicate mathematically versus simply acquiring and supplying one "right solution." Problems that were rooted in the context of students' everyday lives and that required children to reason math-

ematically began to develop, replacing problems that were based on a traditional, textbook-driven curriculum. These changes have resulted in students who value mathematics and are more confident in their abilities to solve mathematical problems in a variety of ways.

The movement in mathematics education to make mathematics even more relevant to students through curriculum connections has included the use of children's literature for mathematics instruction. Teachers have been incorporating into students' investigations quality trade books that have a strong story line but also develop mathematical concepts. Although this source of meaningful mathematics experiences remains largely untapped (Thiessen and Matthias 1992), educational materials and activities are becoming increasingly available. With this realization, I knew that the underlying philosophical support and materials were in place to develop a school lending library that would support mathematics.

Other research influenced my planning. The last two decades have seen an increased emphasis on the use of manipulatives as tools to help children form mathematical concepts and thinking processes. Manipulative use became theoretically justified through the research of Zoltan Dienes and Jerome Bruner in the 1960s. Many studies of the effectiveness of using concrete learning materials have been conducted since then, giving rise to agreement that effective mathematics instruction in the elementary grades incorporates the liberal use of concrete materials (Thompson 1994). Creating hands-on activities for children is beneficial in formulating a knowledge base for mathematical thinking. Therefore, in addition to a system for lending children's books, I incorporated manipulatives into the library to encourage a hands-on approach to any mathematics activities arising from the children's literary activities.

Another concern influenced my thinking in the planning stages of this project. The need for family involvement in student learning is not a new idea; many educators have long understood the importance of the family in educating youth. But these sentiments have not always been emphasized in educational settings. Fortunately, the home-to-school connection to learning is experiencing a resurgence in popular thinking. The United States Department of Education, under Secretary Richard Riley, has strongly advocated family involvement through such reports as *Strong Families, Strong Schools* (1994) and *Employers, Families, and Education: Promoting Family Involvement in Learning* (1994). With so many new methods being incorporated into the mathematics curriculum, it is doubly important to remember the importance of the home-to-school connection. The lending library allowed parents to stay abreast of the changes taking place with the mathematics curriculum and to help them become active participants in the process.

"A Book, a Bed, a Bag: Interactive Home for '10'" (Merenda 1995) and "Literature-Based Math Kits to Take Home" (Burns 1994) also influenced my planning of this project. Merenda's article was a response by a teacher to her kindergarten students' suggestion that she include a mathematics book in their overnight storybook bags. The Burns article featured a librarian and a Chapter-1 mathematics specialist's desire to increase parental involvement in their school's K–2 mathematics program.

Applying the Research: Developing the Project

Mathematics concepts can be taught, emphasized, and explored through literature and manipulatives, as our day-to-day instructional practices at Price Laboratory School (PLS) were already demonstrating. Other questions remained. Would family involvement through reading quality literature with mathematical content further enhance students' learning and attitudes toward mathematics? Would families feel a stronger connection to the elementary school mathematics program through these efforts? Could the steady flow of mathematics materials and books be organized in such a way that all children would have frequent access to a wide range of activities throughout the school year? The Price Laboratory School Mathematics Lending Library was developed to find the answers to these questions.

Year 1 of the project focused on activities that involved the entire elementary school faculty in planning. During this year the faculty participation greatly enriched the ideas that initially launched the project. Even though all faculty members were involved in the big picture of the project, my personal efforts were concentrated in developing the fourth-grade area to troubleshoot potential difficulties. The procedures developed for my grade level helped me direct my colleagues in the second year of the project.

My first step included researching literature titles for grade 4 in the areas of mathematical concepts, as shown in figure 1. Note that activities from all strands of the NCTM's Standards are included. Next I purchased the literature and supporting manipulatives for my own classroom. This purchase showed me the actual cost of acquiring from twenty to thirty books, with supporting materials, for each classroom library. I learned that about $200 could purchase the appropriate number of books for each room, leaving approximately $100 for each class for manipulatives and other supporting resources.

Field-testing the newly acquired fourth-grade lending library was my next step. This trial gave me feedback about the kinds of books and activities that students might enjoy (see fig. 2). As the students delved into the pilot library, they became immersed in playing mathematical games suggested in several books; writing recipes from a children's cookbook; trying out calculator riddles; exploring shapes through pattern grids; and examining the anamorphic adventure featured in Ted Rand's version of Carl Sandburg's (1993) poem "Arithmetic." This small field test proved to be worthwhile for gathering valuable data about ways to maintain high student interest in the project.

Once the initial field-testing data had been gathered, it was time to share this information with the rest of the faculty. We discussed these ideas in two after-school meetings. With the project's goals clearly established, a Saturday shopping spree for faculty was planned. Teachers were able to view and select for purchase appropriate titles for inclusion in their individual classroom libraries. Teachers who were unable to participate in the field trip either reviewed and selected some books brought back for them on approval or ordered them through a catalog (see fig. 3).

As the school year drew to a close, the elementary teachers planned a get-together to reexamine the books they had chosen and select manipulatives to support each piece of literature. This activity was an exciting way for teachers to interact through sharing titles and ideas that brought the literature to life. When the manipulatives were delivered to school over the summer, I was able to connect them with the appropriate class library.

With so much to organize, the project could have become overwhelming. However, I received invaluable volun-

Fourth-Grade Mathematical Concepts, Books, and Manipulatives for Purchase

Concept	Book Title(s)	Manipulative
Money	*All Kinds of Money* *Money*	Play money—coins and bills
Time	*Time* *Anno's Sundial*	Geared student clocks
Number concepts	*I've Got Your Number, John* *The Twelve Circus Rings*	Bucket of base-ten blocks
Place value	*How Much Is a Million?* *Zero Is Something*	Place-value box
Fractions	*Fractions Are Parts of Things*	Fraction squares
Multiplication	*Anno's Mysterious* *Multiplying Jar* *Each Orange Had 8 Slices*	Counting chips
Division	*Esio Trot* *A Remainder of One*	Scale Counting chips
Basic facts	*Mouse Count!* *Number Families*	Bead abacus
Geometry and spatial sense	*The Bedspread* *Grandfather Tang's Story*	Geometric shapes Tangram pieces
Problem solving	*Mr. Grigg's Work* *The 329th Friend*	Double dominoes Counting chips
Measurement	*The King's Giraffe* *The Storybook Cookbook*	Maps Measuring cup and spoons
Reasoning (classification, logic)	*Logic for Space Age Kids* *Tic Tac Toe*	Jumbo foam dice Pattern blocks
Calculators	*Calculator Fun*	Calculators
Technology	*Number Mysteries*	
Cultural connections	*What Time Is It around* *the World?* *Count Your Way*	Clocks

Fig. 1. A fourth-grade inventory, with books listed by curriculum strand

Fig. 2. Diane McCarty discusses one of the books with fourth graders

Fig. 3. A new PLS teacher browses through purchased books.

Fig. 4. Clerical support is provided.

teer clerical assistance to create an inventory of the books and manipulatives for each classroom, as well as a complete list of the entire library (see **fig. 4**). After a few work sessions, the books and accompanying manipulatives were ready to go into plastic carrying bags and hang from sturdy portable stands that could easily be stored in each classroom (see fig. 5).

The Lending Library Is in Place

A few details still needed attention. Labels specifically identifying each item as part of the lending library were placed in the front cover of books as well as on manipulatives. A library check-out system was designed, which resulted in a continuously rotating list of students' names attached to each bag. Individual teachers constructed their own tracking systems so that children could check out a new book each week.

Journals were designed to travel with many of the kits to record each family's mathematical activities on paper in words, pictures, or both. This resource proved valuable not only for the teachers but for the families as well as they generated creative mathematical activities. When the kits were ready to travel, an "in-service program" was conducted by homeroom teachers to entice their students to enjoy the creatively bagged items with their families.

A necessary component of this project was preparing the parents through several avenues. First, a summer newsletter was mailed to every home in our school attendance area to inform parents about this new project. Next, an additional letter was distributed to parents during the opening days of school, personally inviting each family to participate in the project.

An all-school open house was held in mid-September; all rooms were ready with their classroom lending-library kits organized and on display for the parents and children to view and check out. The PLS Mathematics Lending Library was finally officially launched as the kits traveled home with participating families (see fig. 6).

Examples of Lending-Library Selections

The fun began as *One Hundred Hungry Ants* (Pinczes 1993) and creepy plastic ants; *Theodoric's Rainbow* (Kramer 1995) and an acrylic equilateral prism; *People* (Spier 1980) with versatile linking counters in the shape of people; *Kids Make Pizza* recipe book (Buck-Murray 1995) with a pizza pan, measuring cups, and *The King of Pizza* (Sanzari 1995) historical book; *Calculator Riddles* (Adler 1995) and *Just a Minute* (Slater 1996)

with a stopwatch—just to name a few of the almost 300 titles—proceeded out the school's doors.

A title that was thoroughly enjoyed by intermediate grade families, but could be used at any grade level, was *Math in the Bath (and Other Fun Places, Too!)* (Atherlay 1995). The kit included the book, a personal mathematics journal, a bubbles recording booklet, a container of bubble solution, and a wand (see fig. 7). The personal journal highlighted a few questions similar to those posed in the book: (1) Where is mathematics in the morning? (2) Where is mathematics in the classroom? (3) Where is mathematics during physical education? (4) Where is mathematics in the great outdoors? (5) Where is mathematics at supper? (6) Add your own question and answer it. These and other questions were used to stimulate each family's mathematical investigations (see fig. 8).

Families and children had various reactions to the open-ended invitation to be creative in their personal responses to this kit. Some intermediate students designed another rhyming entry for the journal to indicate a new place of discovery in their mathematical observations (e.g., "Math in the Sun Is So Much Fun" and "Math in the Car Can Really Take You Far"). Some parents were amazed at the number of places in which students actually observed mathematics in their own homes!

Developing a Mathematics Lending Library

From my experiences with a lending library for families at the Price Laboratory School, what advice would I offer teachers who are interested in developing a similar program in their own school? The list would be long, but the following points seem particularly valuable.

- Go slowly. Take time to find good mathematics-related literature and supporting activities that

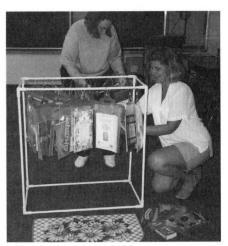

Fig. 5. A completed third-grade kit is examined.

Fig. 6. Mother and son enjoy a book kit, which includes *The Right Number of Elephants* and elephant attribute blocks.

Fig. 7. The complete kit of *Math in the Bath (and Other /Fun Places, Too!)*.

TITLE: *Math in the Bath (and Other Fun Places, Too!)*

Author:	Sara Atherlay
Description:	This book attempts to make mathematics less abstract and make it relevant to students by noting how mathematics is found everywhere and every day in the world around them.
Directions:	Enjoy this book as a family. Use the questions in the journal to discover mathematics at home, in your neighborhood, and at school. Record your mathematical discoveries in the journal. Draw any pictures that will add to our understanding of your investigations. The last page is blank for you to record your own question.
Extra! Extra!:	Bubble solution and wand are included if you desire to create mathematics in the bath, as suggested by the book, or just on your back steps. Count the number of bubbles you can blow with one breath. Compare the size of the smallest and largest to something similar in size. Record your answers in the bubbles recording booklet.
Items in this kit:	1 book 1 personal journal 1 bubble-solution container and wand 1 bubbles recording booklet
ENJOY!	

Fig. 8. The suggested activity directions to use with *Math in the Bath (and Other Fun Places, Too!)*

will be enticing and fun for families to enjoy together.

- Start small. Begin with a few titles, manipulatives, or suggested related activities for just your classroom. The library can always grow to other levels as money and means become available.

- Be creative. Find mathematics everywhere, and let your literature selections and your suggested activities reflect this thought. An atlas has a lot of mathematics, as do science experiments, hopscotch, and magic tricks. Do not limit your ideas, because true mathematical connetions abound all around us.

- Have fun. Be sold on your lending-library concept and implement it wisely, and it will be successful

with students and parents. Involve as many people as you can to spread the workload and increase the opportunities for positive collaborations within your school.

Conclusion

How effective is the mathematics lending library? Various ideas are being implemented to gather such data informally. Teachers and families have reacted positively. Student interest has been high. In addition to the student journals that have been incorporated into many kits, a parent, student, and student survey will be used to gather more feedback at the end of the year (fig. 9).

The "PLS Mathematics Lending Library—Connecting Home" is a project in progress at this time and should enhance the communication of our school's mathematical goals. The faculty at our school will continue "Connecting Home" through our

Please take a few minutes and fill out this survey. Your comments will give us valuable information for the continuation of this project for another year.

Parent Survey of PLS Mathematics Lending Library

1. What did you think of the "PLS Mathematics Lending Library—Connecting Home" when you first heard about it through your newsletter or child? _____

2. What were some of the most positive aspects that your family shared by participating in this project? _____

3. What were some ideas for improvement that occurred to your child or to you during your use of the mathematics lending-library materials? _____

4. In what ways did you see your child grow in his or her mathematical abilities as you worked through the literature selections with your child? _____

THANKS FOR RESPONDING! Please send this survey back to school with your child by _____

Fig. 9. Sample of a parent survey sheet, which is similar to the survey to be used with both students and teachers

existing mathematics program, which incorporates the NCTM's Standards, is activity- and manipulative-based, focuses on developing mathematics concepts, and encourages children's reasoning. The inclusion of children's literature as a vehicle for all areas of an integrated curriculum also makes this lending library a natural extension of our classroom. Parents can now become even more actively involved in our program through activities that will be included in this project.

The total extent of these school-family connections will be challenging to assess because of the potential opportunities that each kit provides to expand students' thinking in various ways. The added dimension of family involvement will stretch the measurement process. However, on the basis of the responses to the lending library at this time, it appears that the project will have a positive impact on our elementary school mathematics program, the students, and their families, regardless of the directions it takes.

References

Adler, David. *Calculator Fun.* New York: Franklin Watts, 1981.

———. *All Kinds of Money.* New York, Franklin Watts, 1984.

———. *Calculator Riddles.* New York: Holiday House, 1995.

Anno, Masaichiro, and Mitsumasa Anno. *Anno's Mysterious Multiplying Jar.* New York: Philomel Books, 1983.

Anno, Mitsumasa. *Anno's Sundial.* New York: Philomel Books, 1987.

Atherlay, Sara. *Math in the Bath (and Other Fun Places, Too!).* New York: Simon & Schuster Books for Young Readers, 1995.

Baumann, Hans. *What Time Is It around the World?* New York: Scroll Press, 1979.

Berg, Olive S. *I've Got Your Number, John.* New York: Holt, Rinehart & Winston, 1965.

Briers, Audrey. *Money.* New York: Franklin Watts, 1987.

Buck-Murray, Marian. *Kids Make Pizza: 40 Fun and Easy Recipes.* Rocklin, Calif.: Prima Publishers, 1995.

Burns, Marilyn. "Literature-Based Math Kits to Take Home." *Instructor Magazine* 103 (April 1994): 42.

Butrick, Lyn McClure. *Logic for Space Age Kids.* Athens, Ohio: University Classics, 1984.

Chwast, Seymour. *The Twelve Circus Rings.* San Diego: Harcourt Brace Jovanovich, 1993.

Collier, Mary Jo, and Peter Collier. *The King's Giraffe.* New York: Simon & Schuster Books for Young Readers, 1996.

Dahl, Roald. *Esio Trot.* New York: Viking, 1990.

Dennis, Richard. *Fractions Are Parts of Things.* New York: Thomas Y. Crowell Co., 1973.

Fair, Sylvia. *The Bedspread.* New York: William Morrow, 1982.

Giganti, Paul. *Each Orange Had 8 Slices: A Counting Book.* New York: Greenwillow Books, 1992.

Haskins, Jim. *Count Your Way through China.* Minneapolis, Minn.: Carolrhoda Books, 1987.

Hayes, Cyril, and Dympna Hayes. *Number Mysteries.* Milwaukee, Wisc.: Penworthy Publishing, 1987.

Kirst, Werner. *Time.* Woodstock, N.Y.: Beekman Publishers, 1997.

Kramer, Stephen. *Theodoric's Rainbow.* New York: Scientific American Books for Young Readers, 1995.

Law, Felicia, and Suzanne Chandler. *Mouse Count!* Milwaukee, Wisc.: Gareth Stevens, 1985.

Luce, Marnie. *Zero Is Something.* Minneapolis, Minn.: Lerner Publications, 1969.

MacGregor, Carol. *The Storybook Cookbook.* Garden City, N.Y.: Doubleday, 1967.

Merenda, Rose C. "A Book, a Bed, and a Bag: Interactive Homework for '10.'" *Teaching Children Mathematics* 1 (January 1995): 288–93.

National Council of Teachers of Mathematics (NCTM). *Curriculum and Evaluation Standards for School Mathematics.* Reston, Va.: NCTM, 1989.

Pinczes, Elinor. *One Hundred Hungry Ants.* Boston: Houghton Mifflin Co., 1993.

———. *A Remainder of One.* Boston: Houghton Mifflin Co., 1995.

Rylant, Cynthia. *Mr. Grigg's Work.* New York: Orchard Books, 1989.

Sandburg, Carl. *Arithmetic.* Illustrated by Ted Rand. San Diego: Harcourt Brace Jovanovich, 1993.

Sanzari, Sylvester. *The King of Pizza: A Magical Story about the World's Favorite Food.* New York: Workman Publishing, 1995.

Schwartz, David M. *How Much Is a Million?* New York: Lothrop, Lee & Shepherd Books, 1985.

Sharmat, Marjorie Weinman. *The 329th Friend.* New York: Four Winds Press, 1979.

Slater, Teddy. *Just a Minute.* New York: Scholastic, 1996.

Speir, Peter. *People.* Garden City, N.Y.: Doubleday, 1980.

Srivastava, Jane Jonas. *Number Families.* New York: Thomas Y. Crowell Co., 1979.

Theissen, Diane, and Margaret Matthias. *The Wonderful World of Mathematics.* Reston, Va.: National Council of Teachers of Mathematics, 1992.

Thompson, Patrick W. "Research into Practice: Concrete Materials and Teaching for Mathematical Understanding." *Arithmetic Teacher* 41 (May 1994): 556–59.

Tompert, Ann. *Grandfather Tang's Story.* New York: Crown Publishers, 1990.

U.S. Department of Education. *Employers, Families, and Education: Promoting Family Involvement in Learning.* Washington, D.C.: U.S. Department of Education, 1994.

———. *Strong Families, Strong Schools.* Washington, D.C.: U.S. Department of Education, 1994.

Viorst, Judith. *Alexander, Who Used to Be Rich Last Sunday.* New York: Aladdin Books, 1978.

Zaslavsky, Claudia. *Tic Tac Toe.* New York: Thomas Y. Crowell Co., 1982.

Using Children's Literature

Teachers may find the following references useful when searching for books that can be used to support literature-based mathematics activities either in the classroom or with families at home.

Bresser, Rusty. *Mathematics and Literature: Grades 4–6.* White Plains, N.Y.: Math Solutions Publications/Cuisenaire Co. of America, 1995. ISBN 0-941355-14-4

Schiro, Michael. *Integrating Children's Literature and Mathematics in the Classroom.* New York: Teachers College Press, 1996. ISBN 0-8077-3565-5

Thiessen, Diane, Margaret Matthias, and Jacquelin Smith. *The Wonderful World of Mathematics: A Critically Annotated List of Children's Books in Mathematics.* Reston, Va.: National Council of Teachers of Mathematics, 1998. ISBN 0-87353-439-5

Welchman-Tischler, Rosamond. *How to Use Children's Literature to Teach Mathematics.* Reston, Va.: National Council of Teachers of Mathematics, 1992. ISBN 0-87353-349-6.

Part 3

Family Participation in Home Settings

MATHEMATICS
BACKPACKS:
MAKING THE H0ME-SCHOOL CONNECTION

Sheryl A. Orman

I don't understand how you are teaching math."

"How come we rarely see math worksheets?"

"Why does my child want me to buy craft sticks and beans?"

"You tell me not to use flashcards, but how can I help my child learn math?"

Last year as I began to use various manipulatives with my second graders, I realized that their parents lacked knowledge of current instructional techniques in mathematics. Even though I had displayed objects at our open house and had demonstrated their use when holding conferences with parents, the parents needed more experience with this way of learning.

I also realized that I was ignoring a valuable link to the success of the students' learning. If I could get the parents to understand my methods, I knew that they could also help their children succeed in mathematics.

So I decided to develop something that would help the students teach their families while also furthering their own understanding of mathematics concepts. If parents became actively involved in their children's learning, then both the parents and students would benefit.

I adapted an idea from a reading journal (Reutzel and Fawson 1990). The article explained how first graders

Sheryl Orman teaches fifth grade at Washington Elementary School in Wauwatosa, WI 53213. She is interested in creating activities that integrate curriculum areas and make school learning interesting.

Backpacks bring parents and children together in entertaining learning activities.

took turns taking home a backpack containing various materials to encourage writing activities among family members. I began creating a mathematics backpack with similar goals in mind.

While developing the backpack, I had three main goals:

1. To strengthen the home-school connection by affording opportunities for my students and their families to engage in mathematical activities

2. To present open-ended activities that encourage discussion

3. To develop activities that would be motivating enough to be taken out of the backpack

The result was two different backpacks. Each pack contained a calcula-

tor, markers, pencils, a pad of white paper, a letter of information (see fig. 1), an inventory of the contents, and a mathematics journal for families to record thoughts or reactions. Each pack then had four different activities with individual instructions.

A sample activity, "Toothpicky Patterns," is included in figure 2. This activity requires one person to make a pattern and the other person to add to it. It also includes a suggestion to look for patterns around the house. The idea of parents and children creating the patterns at home together was new and exciting. One mother and daughter said that they had toothpick patterns all over the floor of their living room.

This patterning activity, along with all the other activities in the packs,

Dear _____'s Family,

It is your turn to have mathematics backpack _____. We hope you are ready for lots of fun and learning.

The backpack contains several different mathematics activities. Each one includes directions and necessary materials.

These activities are meant to be done in a family setting. Sisters, brothers, grandmothers, grandfathers, aunts, uncles, moms, and dads should be included.

The purpose of these activities is to help children acquire a better grasp of some mathematics concepts and enjoy working with their family.

THE CHILDREN WILL GET MUCH MORE FROM THE ACTIVITIES IF DISCUSSION ABOUT THE ACTIVITIES OCCURS WHILE THEY ARE TAKING PLACE. DOING ONE ACTIVITY WITH GOOD MATHEMATICS DISCUSSION IS BETTER THAN DOING FIVE ACTIVITIES WITH NO DISCUSSION!

Please check the inventory list to make sure that all materials that arrive at your house are in the backpack when you return it to school. If you misplace or lose any items, please write a note so that we can replace them if possible. Remember, this backpack is for everyone. Please take care and treat it with respect.

Please return this backpack to school on _____ with some comments written in the mathematics log.

Enjoy!

Fig. 1. Draft of letter to be sent home

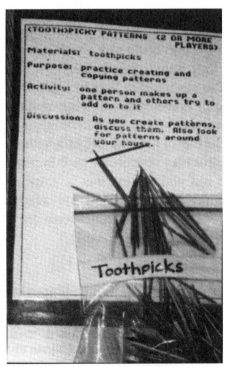

Fig. 2. A sample activity

The mathematics backpacks were shared on a rotating basis in which each student was permitted to keep a pack for two or three days. An information letter went home with the backpack, including the date when the pack should be returned. When the student brought back the pack, he or she was encouraged to share with the class a favorite activity or something interesting that occurred with the backpack activities.

A suggestion from another second-grade teacher has helped me maintain a check on the contents of the backpacks. The student who has just returned the pack sits down with the next student who is going to be taking the pack home, and they review the inventory sheet. Giving the students this responsibility also offers one more chance for mathematically based discussions to develop.

Throughout the process I was pleased to discover that the backpacks did meet my three initial goals. The anticipation of the students as I drew names out of a basket to see who would get to take the backpacks home next and the stories they shared with their classmates when they returned let me know that the activities were being used by the families and that everyone was having fun. Furthermore, the comments written by parents and students in the journals (see fig. 4) gave me the knowledge and satisfaction that the backpacks were a success.

gave families a place to start. From this point, a wide range of ideas and activities could develop.

Laminated graphs and erasable markers were furnished for the activity "Goodness Gracious, Great Graphs." One graph requires the student to sit with a family member looking out a window for ten minutes collecting data and recording it on the graph. They graph the number of cars, trucks, people, bicycles, and animals that pass (see fig. 3). In another activity the student asks various people in the family about the number of hours each usually sleeps and records this information on a graph. Both activities included questions for discussion.

Also included in the backpacks were a subtraction game, an addition game, patterning-block activities, a place-value game, a measurement activity using Unifix cubes, and time-telling activities.

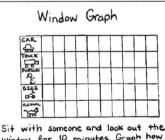

Fig. 3. What do you see out the window?

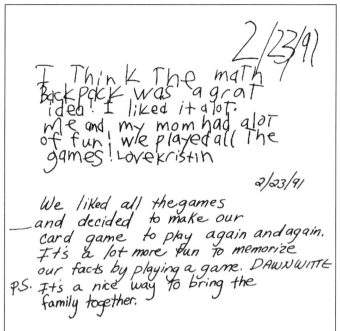

2/23/91

I Think The math Backpack was a grat idea! I liked it a lot. me and my mom had a lot of fun! we played all The games! Love kristin

2/23/91

We liked all the games and decided to make our card game to play again and again. It's a lot more fun to memorize our facts by playing a game. DAWN WITTE PS. It's a nice way to bring the family together.

Fig. 4. One family's reaction

Table 1

Guidelines for developing mathematics backpacks

1. Initially pick three or four areas of mathematics to address in a backpack, preferably in an integrated manner. This variety gives continual exposure to material already covered and can introduce new concepts in an exploratory way.

2. Develop or adapt commercial ideas that present open-ended, motivating activities.

3. Design activities that encourage the interaction of two or more people.

4. Furnish calculators, markers, crayons, paper, pencils, and a journal as standard equipment.

5. Include some questions with each activity's instruction sheet to guide the discussion. These questions should extend the activity to various other situations.

6. Duplicate a form letter to send home explaining the backpack and noting the date on which it should be returned.

7. Include an inventory sheet.

These backpacks can be used across a wide age range. Although I began this activity when I was teaching second grade, I am now teaching fifth grade and am in the process of developing backpacks for this class. The guidelines in table 1 may be helpful to readers with their classes.

The backpacks do not require expensive manipulatives. The patterning blocks in my backpacks were cut from colored mesh plastic canvas by one of the parents. The base-ten blocks were paper models. Sticks and beans would also work. The materials were packaged in sandwich-sized plastic bags that zip shut. Each bag was labeled with the name of the corresponding game.

After the teacher has developed a number of activities, the contents of the backpack can be varied. During particular units the teacher may want to include activities focusing on that topic. Perhaps later in the year students could pick which four activities they want to take home.

The mathematics backpacks furnish the kind of homework that is appropriate for elementary school students: engaging and interactive. They can help strengthen the home-school connection by bringing parents and children together in entertaining learning activities. They are adaptable, enriching, and truly educational for both students and their families.

Bibliography

O'Connell, Susan R. "Math Pairs—Parents as Partners'" *Arithmetic Teacher* 40 (September 1992): 10–12.

Reutzel, D. Ray, and Parker C. Fawson. "Traveling Tales: Connecting Parents and Children through Writing." *Reading Teacher* 44 (November 1990): 222–27.

PARENTS
CAN HELP CHILDREN LEARN MATHEMATICS

Robert B. Ashlock

All parents want their children to enjoy school and succeed with schoolwork. They are eager to help children learn mathematics, but many are not sure how to proceed.

Parents can help children with mathematics if we suggest activities and sample questions to ask. They can help children develop mathematical concepts and build vocabulary, and they can foster an attitude of curiosity about numbers and shapes.

The suggestions that follow can be shared with parents of both preschool children and children in the elementary grades. The suggestions are merely idea starters. Parents will be able to elaborate; they will soon extend the list with their own ideas.

Before you give these activities to a child's parents, highlight those activities for which the child is ready. Even so, parents will also need to judge what is appropriate for each child. Alert them to the fact that they may get some surprises: some children will show understanding beyond what parents expect; others will lack needed skills. These discrepancies can be discussed at the next parent-teacher conference.

Guidelines for Parents

Parents who want to help young children learn may appreciate a few words of guidance. Share some or all of the following guidelines with them.

Robert Ashlock teaches at Covenant College, Lookout Mountain, TN 37350. He is especially interested in helping children who experience difficulty learning mathematics.

1. *Introduce mathematics vocabulary while children are working with objects, pictures, and drawings.* Thereby, new mathematics words will have meaning. Children will develop needed mental pictures for quantities and shapes.

2. *Show personal interest in children's activities that involve number and shape.* Do some of the listed activities with them. Let them know you are excited that they are learning about numbers and shapes. Value highly whatever progress children make in learning mathematics.

3. *Whenever children count, measure, or collect other quantitative information, encourage them to make a record of what they find.* They may select or write numerals, make simple graphs, or possibly make drawings. Sometimes they can make a book that records different stages in a project—complete with pictures. For preschool children, post a record of what the children find out as they count and measure; include a title for the display. Even the child who does not yet read words or numerals will understand that the numerals are a record of "how many," and the words tell about what they did.

4. *Play mathematics games with your children.* One example of a mathematics game for young children is "How many did I take?" (fig. 1). Be sure to take turns.

Activity Descriptions

Children can be involved in mathematics activities in varied settings at home, both indoors and outdoors. The lists of suggested activities that follow

How Many Did I Take?

The first player matches two sets of objects one-to-one and shows that both sets have the same number of objects. While the other player closes his eyes, the first player scrambles all the objects together, then removes some from one set. The other player finds how many were removed by pairing the sets again.

A variation of the game uses only one set of objects, possibly a set of seven marbles. The first player covers part of the set with his hand and has the other player tell how many are under the hand. The objects are then uncovered to see if the number given by the other player is correct.

Fig. 1

are organized by settings so that parents can more easily integrate mathematics with the child's other activities.

Mathematical content is noted for each activity to make it easier for parents to keep mathematical learning in mind as the child proceeds. It is important that interaction with the child be relaxed, at the child's level of development, and undertaken in a spirit of inquiry.

Because children will learn only what they are developmentally ready to learn, activities have been labeled or preschool, grades 1–3, and grades 4–6. However, in any one area of mathematics an individual may be ready for an activity indicated at an earlier or later level.

At the Toy Box

Preschool children can do the following:

* Count toys while putting them away, and then say, "We put away (number) toys."
  Cardinal numbers

* Sort toys into sets: cars, blocks, dolls, and so on. Prepare three-inch-by-five-inch cards with numerals on them and have the child choose a card or each set to show how many items are included. A zero card can be used to show there are no toys of a certain kind.
  Classifying; cardinal numbers; digits

Children in grades 1–3 can do the following:

* Find two-dimensional geometric shapes indicated on toys: squares, circles, rectangles, and other figures. Help the child trace each shape with a finger.
  Plane figures

Ask these questions:

* Which is larger? Which is largest? Which is smaller? Which is smallest?
  Comparing sizes

* Are there more horses or more riders? Are there fewer horses or fewer riders? Match horses and riders one-to-one.
  More than; fewer than

* How many corners are on this block? How many edges?
  Describing solid figures

* Which blocks are shaped like this

one? On blocks and other toys feel and describe flat surfaces, curved surfaces, edges, and corners.
  Describing solid figures

In the Kitchen and the Dining Room

Even young children can help with activities in these rooms. Preschool children can do the following:

* Sort silverware into sets of knives, forks, and spoons.
  Classifying

* Place a paper napkin at the left of each plate. Fold napkins as rectangles one day, then as triangles the next.
  Matching; plane figures

* Compare pots and other containers in the kitchen. Ask, "Which hold most? Which holds least?"
  Comparing volumes

* Order pots by size. Order cans by diameter.
  Ordering

* Find the number of chairs needed to match places set at the dining table.
  Matching; cardinal numbers

Children in grades 1–3 can do the following:

* Count the number of plates, glasses, and so on, to carry to the dining table.
  Cardinal numbers

* Count beans. Ask, "How many beans are in the bowl?"
  Cardinal numbers

* Find how many juice cans of water it takes to fill a pot.
  Cardinal numbers; measuring volume

Children in grades 4–6 can do the following:

* Compute how much of an item is needed to prepare for a meal, given the amount for each person.
  Fractions; multiplying

* Compute the amount needed if a recipe is doubled, tripled, or halved.
  Fractions; multiplying

Around the House

Children can do many things around the house that involve mathematics.

Preschool children can do the following:

- Sort one kind of item (socks, sheets of construction paper, etc.) by size, color, or other quality. Describe individual items.

    Classifying; describing

Children in grades 1–3 can do the following:

- Count on a calendar. Ask, "How many days (weeks, months) until ... ?"

    Cardinal numbers; calendar

- Count the number of containers of water it takes to fill the aquarium.

    Measuring volume

- Make decorations from cutout shapes.

    Plane figures

- Play games that involve counting: games with dice, dominoes, and board games.

    Cardinal numbers

- Find specific pages in the book before story time.

    Numeration

- Estimate, then count the number of people in a room.

    Estimating; counting

- Keep records of weight and height; make a graph and keep it current. Find differences from time to time.

    Measuring length and weight; graphing; subtracting

- Measure things around the house and record the observed measurements. Use metric measurements whenever possible.

    Metric measurement

- Play store, or really sell some product (lemonade, radishes from the garden, etc.). Make change, pay overhead, and calculate profit or loss.

    Problem solving; adding; subtracting

Children in grades 4–6 can do the following:

- Read schedules for information: the television guide; and bus, train, or plane schedules.

    Reading charts

- Estimate the length, width, and area of a room by pacing it off.

    Estimating length and area

- Draw objects they see rather than copy drawings from a book. Give attention to proportion.

    Ratios

- Measure amounts for cooking.

    Fractions; measuring

- Estimate the amount of paint needed for painting a certain area.

    Estimating area

- Build something from a craft book.

    Measuring

In the Garden

Preschool children can do the following:

- Compare flowers. Ask, "Which flower is largest? Which is smallest?"

    Comparing

Children in grades 1–3 can do the following:

- Compare different paths. Ask, "Which path is longer? Which is shorter?"

    Comparing lengths

- Count the number of petals on individual flowers. Ask, "Do all tulips have the same number of petals? Which kind of flower has the greatest number of petals?"

    Counting; comparing numbers

- Find the third plant in the row, then the eighth.

    Ordinal numbers

- Use names of shapes to describe beds of plants.

    Plane figures

Children in grades 4–6 can do the following:

- Find parallel rows of plants.

    Parallel lines

- Keep records of the number of seeds planted and the number of vegetables harvested, then compare ratios for different kinds of vegetables.

    Comparing ratios

In the Yard or at the Playground

Mathematics activities should involve what children see and touch around them.

Preschool children can do the following:

- Order sticks by length "like stairsteps" from shortest to longest, then longest to shortest.

    Ordering lengths

Children in grades 1–3 can do the following:

- Count by twos, fives, and tens when playing hide-and-seek.

    Skip counting; multiples

- Estimate and count pebbles. Ask, "How many pebbles are in a handful?"

    Estimating; cardinal numbers

- Estimate and count leaves. Ask, "How many leaves can we put in this box?"

    Estimating; cardinal numbers

- Compare heights and other lengths.

    Comparing lengths

- Count jumps when jumping with a rope.

    Cardinal numbers

- Count the number of times they are able to bounce the ball without stopping.

    Cardinal numbers

Children in grades 4–6 can do the following:

- Measure the distance they can throw a ball.

  Measuring lengths

- Compare temperatures at different times, or at the same time each day. Make a graph of the temperatures.

  Temperatures; graphing

- Estimate the total number of blades of grass in the yard by measuring, counting blades in small, scattered samples, and multiplying.

  Measuring area; sampling; dividing and multiplying

In the Car

Many activities involve mathematics that children can do while riding in a car.

Preschool children can do the following:

- Name places they have already seen during the ride and name these places in the order they were seen.

  Ordering

Children in grades 1–3 can do the following:

- Count forward to a designated number, or count backward.

  Counting

- Count from 0 to 9 using digits seen on license plates.

  Counting; digits

- Look at house numbers on one side of the street and count by twos.

  Skip counting; multiples

- Read posted route numbers. Find the greatest and the smallest number.

  Numerals; comparing numbers

- Read license plate numbers.

  Numerals

- Add all the digits on license plates and record each sum. Find as great a sum as possible.

  Adding

- Read number of miles to your destination as posted, check the odometer, and occasionally determine the remaining distance.

  Subtracting

Children in grades 4–6 can do the following:

- Play "buzz." All players count together by ones, but they say "buzz" for each multiple of a designated number and for each numeral that contains the designated number. For example, if the number is 3, the count would be the following: 1, 2, buzz, 4, 5, buzz, 7, 8, buzz, 10, 11, buzz, buzz, 14, ….

  Counting; numeration

- Add points for the things the children see. Have each of two children take a side of the car. In one game children collect points for different animals they see: birds count 1 point each; dogs, cows, and cats, 5 points; horses, 10 points; a cat in a window, 100 points. In the city, assign point values to different kinds of signs.

  Adding

- Compute mileage for a trip. Estimate beforehand from a highway map. Also estimate the amount of fuel needed.

  Estimating, adding, dividing

At a Store or a Restaurant

Preschool children can do the following:

- Compare boxes or cans. Ask, "Which box is larger? Which is smaller?"

  Comparing volumes

Children in grades 1–3 can do the following:

- Determine the amount saved from buying things on sale.

  Subtracting

- Select an item to buy and save for it. Ask, "How much money do you have now? How much more do you need to save? How long will it take if you save (so much) each week?"

  Subtracting, multiplying

- Pay for items bought, and show that the change is correct.

  Making change

Children in grades 4–6 can do the following:

- Compare prices and quantities for different brands. Determine which costs less per unit of measure.

  Comparing ratios

- Estimate the amount that will appear on the bill.

  Estimating sums

In the Neighborhood and Beyond

Preschool children can do the following:

- Classify such objects as pebbles, acorns, shells, and leaves. Classify different types or different colors, or use such categories as shiny and dull.

  Classifying

- Find the second house from the corner, then the fourth.

  Ordinal numbers

- Compare scores at a game to see who is ahead.

  Comparing numbers

- Keep score in a game. Add or subtract as needed.

  Adding; subtracting; comparing numbers

• Look for one or more of the following while taking a walk. Be sure to take special note of signs, buildings, and other construction projects.

—Triangles, squares and other rectangles, hexagons, octagons, and so on. (The roofs of houses include different shapes.)

Plane figures

—Different quadrilaterals: rectangle, parallelogram, trapezoid, rhombus, and so on.

Quadrilaterals

—Parallel lines

Parallel lines

• Inventory different kinds of pets in the neighborhood, and make a bar graph to show the number of each kind.

Graphs

• Make a list of the birthdays of family and friends and then put the dates in sequence. Make a bar graph to show the number of birthdays each month.

Graphs

• Open a savings account, and keep track of interest earned and the balance.

Adding; percent

• Keep bowling scores and find averages.

Adding; averages

• Compute batting averages of baseball players.

Decimals; dividing

Conclusion

Share these activity descriptions with parents. Or, let these descriptions stimulate your own thinking; describe activities that are particularly appropriate for your students to do in *their* homes, and share your ideas with parents.

Parents *can* help young children learn mathematics. They can help children see number and shape in the world around them. They can help children understand the importance and usefulness of mathematics.

Bibliography

For teachers
Bloom, Benjamin S. *All Our Children Learning: A Primer for Parents, Teachers, and Other Educators.* New York: McGraw-Hill Book Co., 1981. See especially chapters 4 ("Early Learning in the Home") and 5 ("The Effect of the Home Environment on Children's School Achievement").

Gotts, Edward E., and Richard F. Purnell. *Improving Home School Communications.* Fastback #230. Bloomington, Ind.: Phi Delta Kappa Educational Foundation, 1985.

Phi Delta Kappa. "Parent Involvement in Education." *Practical Applications of Research* 4 (December 1981). Newsletter of Phi Delta Kappa's Center of Evaluation, Development, and Research.

Scheer, Janet K., and Michael T. Henninger. "Math Clinic: An Ideal Setting for Parent Involvement." *Arithmetic Teacher* 30 (October 1982): 48–51.

For parents
Chapey, Geraldine. *Ready for School: How Parents Can Prepare Children for School Success.* Lanham, Md.: University Press of America, 1986.

Flexer, Roberta J., and Carolyn L. Topping "Mathematics on the Home Front." *Arithmetic Teacher* 36 (October 1988): 12–19.

Karnes, Merle B. *Learning Mathematical Concepts at Home.* Reston, Va.: Council for Exceptional Children, 1980.

Morse, Philip S. *Home-Style Learning: Activities for Young Children and Their Parents.* Englewood Cliffs, N.J.: Prentice-Hall, 1981. See especially chapter 5.

Reys, Barbara. *Elementary School Mathematics: What Parents Should Know about Estimation.* Reston, Va.: National Council of Teachers of Mathematics, 1982.

———. *Elementary School Mathematics: What Parents Should Know about Problem Solving.* Reston, Va.: National Council of Teachers of Mathematics, 1982.

Rich, Dorothy, and Cynthia Jones. *The Three R's Plus: Teaming Families and Schools for Student Achievement.* Washington, D.C.: The Home and School Institute, 1978.

TABLE-TOP MATHEMATICS—

A HOME-STUDY PROGRAM FOR EARLY CHILDHOOD

**Marilyn Sue Ford
and Caroline
Gibson Crew**

When parents come into the kindergarten or first-grade classroom for their first conference, the teacher often hears one of two concerns: "How can I help my child at home?" and "I can't work

Marilyn Ford is an assistant professor in the Department of Curriculum and Instruction at the University of Nevada, Las Vegas, NV 89154. She teaches undergraduate and graduate courses in elementary mathematics education. As a teacher-educator, she is interested in the development and implementation of developmentally appropriate K–6 mathematics curricula. Caroline Crew teaches at Hatfield Elementary School in Hatfield, PA 19440. She is interested in the use of manipulatives for cognitive development.

with my child at home; it's too frustrating." Coming from parents who have little or no experience in the teaching of young children, these statements are valid and understandable. First, parents often do not know what to do to assist their child in extending the classroom learning at home. Their attempt is often directed back to the teacher by asking for extra worksheets to be completed after school. However, the young child who has worked hard at school should not be expected to return home, sit down, and do worksheets. Children should be allowed a time to relax, just as adults require after a day at work. Homework should be in the form of an activity similar to

the developmental, hands-on learning experiences used in the classroom.

Second, working with one's own child can be very difficult, even for teachers! When the parent becomes frustrated, the child often feels like a failure, and the attempt to help may end in tears. Bristor (1987) speculates that some parents' frustration may come from a belief that "only the specially trained can do a particular job well" (p. 23). Yet, she states, parents have been helping their children learn language, social skills, and other behaviors prior to coming to school. With guidance, parents can become confident in working with their child at home.

Home-Study Program

It is important that teachers encourage and solicit parents' help with young children. Recent research indicates that significant academic improvement results from parents' active involvement in a home-study program (Bristor 1987; Bennett 1986; Croft 1979). Helping parents set up a home-assistance program can easily be accomplished with forethought and organization.

The idea for the "Table-Top Mathematics" program was developed after one author's experience of standing over her child expectantly, waiting for her to complete a task, too quickly offering help (which was more like interference), and finally coming to realize what students' parents had been saying all these years.

Table-top-mathematics tasks are simple activities that can be completed by a pupil at the kitchen table while the parent cooks or does chores nearby. This approach alleviates the problem of the parent's sitting close by watching in anticipation. The game-like activities are simple and quick, so the child can complete a number of them in a short time. Materials for the activities can be collected and stored in a "mathematics box" for easy access. These materials are inexpensive and often found around the house. Activity sheets for table-top math can be sent home monthly to stimulate students' interest, coordinate the home-based program with the classroom curriculum, or serve as review for all students.

During the first parent-teacher conference of the year, explain the program to the parent and send home the materials list for the mathematics box, along with the first activity sheet. Recommend a fifteen- to twenty-minute work period four times a week. The time and frequency can be increased by the pupil or parents. Remind parents that setting a time for homework helps establish a routine.

The parent begins the home-study session by choosing an activity and telling the child which materials are needed, then explains the task. If the activity is difficult or is being done for the first time, the parent can do an example with the child. The parent should then allow the child to work independently. When the child is finished, the parent checks the work. Parents may find that the more sophisticated activities, such as adding and subtracting, require more supervision and uninterrupted time with the child.

One skill can be emphasized during each work session by repeating variations of the same activity or by choosing two or three sequential activities. Stress to the parent that although the child should be encouraged to complete a task assigned, if he or she begins to show signs of frustration, a compliment should be given on the work completed and the work session ended. Parents may choose to keep a calendar chart of the days on which table-top mathematics was completed (see fig. 1). Children can apply a small sticker or star to the calendar chart each time they finish a session. The parent can indicate which activity was completed, and the child can rate it. Activities that the child enjoys can be repeated at various times. On completion of a monthly chart, children and parents can celebrate with a special lunch (try ordering by number!), a trip to the library to look for mathematics-related books, or an outing of the child's choice. Encourage the parents to be creative and have fun—they deserve it!

The following home-study program, designed as handouts, is written for the parent. The handouts include a list of collectible materials for a mathematics box, as well as activity sheets addressing the mathematical topics of sorting, patterning, counting and numbers, geometry, adding, subtracting, and measuring. Each activity sheet describes a series of simple tasks related to one of the topics. The sequence of tasks increases in difficulty and

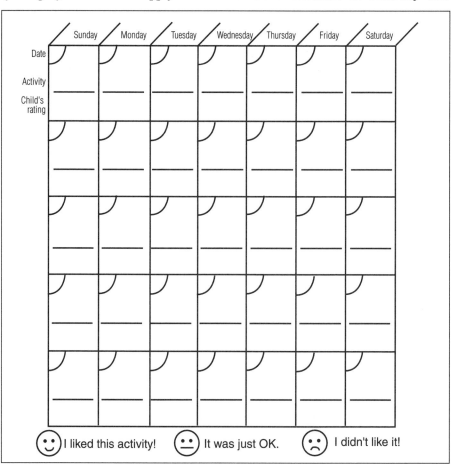

Fig. 1. Calendar chart

ends with extension ideas for parents to continue their children's learning beyond the table top.

Materials for the mathematics box

Use a large shirt box or other type of box with a lid to store materials. During one session, allow your child to decorate the box. The lid can be outlined with a pattern of beans or macaroni. Numerals can be written with white glue and sprinkled with rice or cornmeal. When dry, the numerals can be traced with fingers to reinforce correct formation (see fig. 2). Use reclosable plastic bags or plastic containers to keep the loose materials separate. Encourage your child to pack the materials neatly when finished.

The box should include the following materials:

- Approximately twenty to thirty buttons of different sizes, colors, and types
- Macaroni in various shapes—elbows, rigatoni, shells, and so on
- At least three different kinds of beans—lima beans, brown beans, kidney beans, and so on
- Rice or cornmeal
- Clay
- Various lengths of colored yarn scraps, ribbon, or shoelaces
- A write-on-wipe-off message board with erasable pen
- Five to ten small paper or plastic plates
- Flashcards or index cards with the numerals 1–20

Have available for use paper, crayons, scissors, white glue, and old magazines to be cut up.

Sorting activities

Sorting, or classifying, is a very basic and enjoyable mathematics skill at which children aged four years or older can be very successful. Any collection of items can be sorted into groups by color, size, shape, use, or texture. Sorting activities need not be limited to materials in the mathematics box; household items can also be used. Allow your child time to handle the objects to be sorted. Give your child the opportunity to verbalize the reasons for sorting as he or she did.

- Combine all the macaroni shapes in a bowl. Mix them up. Ask your child to sort the macaroni pieces onto the paper plates so that each plate has only one kind of macaroni. Try the same activity with the beans.

- Pick out one button. Have your child tell about the button-the size, color, number of holes, and so on. Ask her or him to find all the buttons that are like that button in one way. For example, find all the buttons with two holes, all the blue buttons, all the large buttons.

- Lay out the paper plates. Ask your child to sort the buttons onto the paper plates so that all the buttons on each plate are alike in one way.

Have your child explain how the buttons are alike.

- Ask your child to sort the yarn pieces or shoelaces onto the paper plates. Have your child explain how they are sorted when finished, for example, by color, thickness, length, and so on.

Extensions: Encourage your child to help sort the laundry and match and roll socks together. Have your child put away the silverware, each piece in its own section.

Patterning activities

Mathematics is based on patterns. As mathematics skills become more abstract, the patterns involved may be more difficult to recognize. Therefore, it is necessary to allow children the opportunity to recognize, copy, extend, and create patterns at an early age, as well as throughout elementary school. As you work with your child on patterns, she or he will

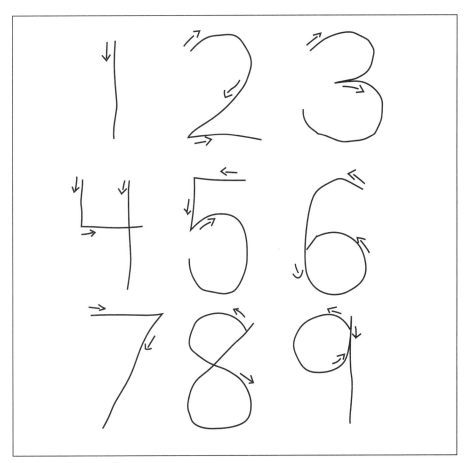

Fig. 2. The correct way to write numerals

begin to recognize patterns every-where! Children will soon be able to use materials of all sorts to create patterns.

- Make a pattern with two different types of beans. Begin with a simple pattern such as white, red; white, red; ... (see [a] in fig. 3). Have your child copy the pattern using the same types of beans. Try other two-bean patterns (see [b] in fig. 3).

- Start a six-bean pattern, using two different types of beans. Ask your child to say the pattern, copy the pattern, and then extend it using up to twenty more beans. Check the pattern by reciting the color or name.

- Make a pattern using two different types of beans. Have your child copy and extend the pattern. Then, using paper and crayons, have your child draw and color the pattern on paper.

- Have your child try making patterns using two different types of maca-roni or buttons. Ask your child to say the pattern.

- Patterns can become more challenging by using more types of similar objects (see [c] in fig. 3). Encourage your child to repeat the foregoing activities using three or more kinds of similar objects.

Extensions: During a walk with your child, pick up some leaves, sticks, and pebbles to use for a pattern picture. While in the car, recite a verbal pattern: "Red, red, blue, blue; red, red, blue, blue. Say it with me."

Counting and number activities

Children sometimes begin counting at an early age, by mimicking older siblings or characters on "Sesame Street." Early experiences should help your child make the connection between counting and the actual number symbol. Children need to be able to count three objects, know that three are in the set, and identify the symbol that represents a quantity of three. The following activities emphasize counting and identifying numerals. Allow time for your child to explore and get a feel for numbers.

- Count every day with your child. Begin by counting to ten together. When he or she can count to ten alone without mistakes, extend your counting to fifteen, then to twenty, and so on. If your child makes mistakes, simply correct him or her and go on. When your child can say the numbers in order, have her or him count small piles of beans or macaroni and tell you how many are in the pile.

- Using the numeral flashcards with see-and-say repetition, begin working on recognizing the numerals 1–5. When your child can recognize and name these numerals out of order, go on to 1–10.

- Have your child make numerals out of clay. Lay out a numeral flashcard or refer to a "rice" numeral on the mathematics-box lid. Have your child trace the numeral (see fig. 2) with his or her finger. Ask your child to make a "snake" by rolling out the clay and then use the snake to form the numeral. Be sure the child can identify the numeral name before she or he tries another one.

- Cover the bottom of a paper plate with rice or cornmeal. Show your child a numeral, then have him or her say it and write it in the rice using one finger.

- Hide the flashcards around the room and ask your child to go on a "number hunt." As the child finds a numeral card, have him or her hand it to you, say the number name, and continue hunting.

- Lay six buttons on one plate, eight on another, and three on another. Ask your child to count the number of buttons on each plate and find the numeral card that goes with each plate. Or, put one numeral flashcard on each of the three plates. Ask your child to place the number of beans on each plate to match the flashcard.

Extensions: Have your child help set the table by counting people, plates, forks, and so on. Take a trip to the library to find number-rhyme books. Learn number rhymes and songs together.

Geometry activities

Shapes are everywhere! Young children need to recognize, name, and describe various simple shapes. Try to use the names of shapes when talking with your child, for instance, say,

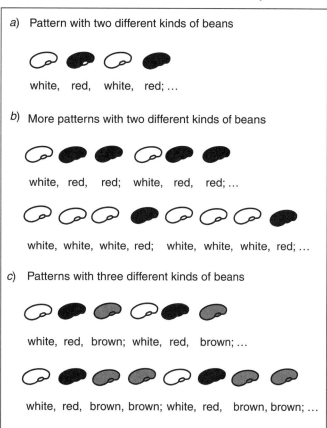

a) Pattern with two different kinds of beans

white, red, white, red; ...

b) More patterns with two different kinds of beans

white, red, red; white, red, red; ...

white, white, white, red; white, white, white, red; ...

c) Patterns with three different kinds of beans

white, red, brown; white, red, brown; ...

white, red, brown, brown; white, red, brown, brown; ...

Fig 3. Bean patterns

"Bring me the rectangular pot holder" or "What shape is this cookie?" Help your child see the shapes in different objects. Start with the three basic shapes: circle, rectangle, and triangle. As your child becomes comfortable with these, add oval, diamond, pentagon, and others.

- Cut out the shapes from the geometry handouts (see fig. 4). Lay down the figures tilting some of them. Ask your child to sort the shapes into groups. When she or he has finished, say together, "Here is a group of circles," or "This is a group of rectangles." You may want your child to count the number of shapes in each group and say, "Five circles, five triangles," and so on.

- Ask your child to use the shapes to make a picture. The shapes can become a house, a person, a truck—almost anything. You may need to try one together first as an example. Have your child tell about the shape picture.

- Have your child flatten clay and cut out shapes using geometric cookie cutters or a plastic knife.

- Pour a layer of rice on a paper plate. Ask your child to draw a shape in the rice, shake it for a fresh surface, and repeat with another shape. Have your child say the name of each shape while drawing.

- Have your child use the shape cutouts to make a pattern, such as circle, triangle, rectangle; circle, triangle, rectangle; … ; then ask your child to draw the shape pattern on paper.

Extensions: Point out shapes in the environment as you are walking or driving, especially road signs and business logos. Remember to have your child name and describe the shapes.

Addition activities

You may have heard your child say, "One plus one is two" and assumed your child knows how to add. The

Teacher: Copy these shapes onto two different colors of construction paper to send home.
Parent: Carefully cut out these shapes for your child.

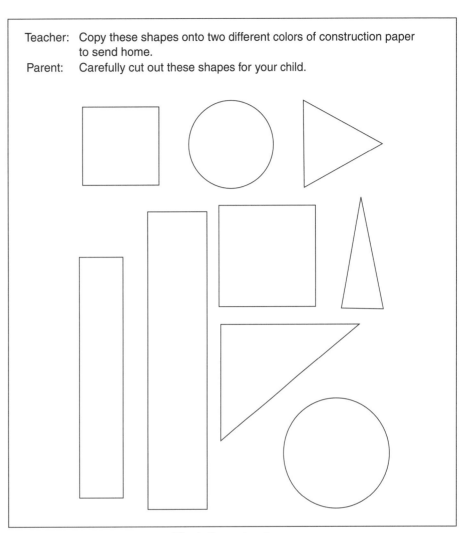

Fig. 4. Geometry shapes

process of addition entails much more than memorizing the addition facts. Hands-on experiences help your child understand that addition is a process of putting things together. To help your child master this skill, be sure he or she shows the work using objects.

- Introduce adding with the concept of "one more." Place one bean on a section of a paper plate. Ask your child to put one more bean on the plate. Move the beans together, then say aloud, "One bean plus one bean equals two beans." Ask your child to repeat the sentence. Next say, "Two beans are on the plate. Now add one more bean." When your child places another bean on the plate, have her or him push the beans together and say, "Two beans plus one more bean equals three beans." Continue adding one more until you have ten beans on the plate.

- Lay out two numeral flashcards. Have your child put the correct number of buttons under each card. Ask, "How many would we have if we put them together?" Have your child push the buttons together, count them, and then find the numeral flashcard for the sum (see [a] in fig. 5). (Make certain that the sum will be less than 21.)

- Encourage your child to add by counting on from a set. If shown piles of three and two buttons, the child says, "Three," and continues counting, "Four, five," while moving the pile of two buttons one at a time over to the pile of three (see [b] in fig. 5).

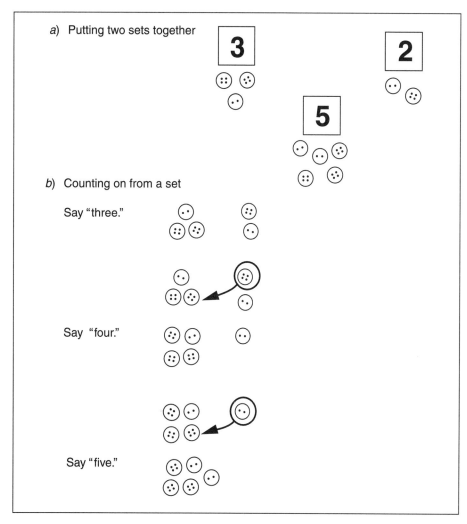

a) Putting two sets together

b) Counting on from a set

Say "three."

Say "four."

Say "five."

Fig. 5. Adding sets

- Write on the erasable board a number problem, such as 2 + 5 = [ ]. Have your child work out the problem using beans. Encourage him or her to tell a number story while counting out and adding the beans.

- Set up a number problem with the beans. Have your child write the corresponding number problem on the erasable board and then find the answer.

Extensions: Use number stories whenever possible. "Two people are ready for dinner. Two more people joined them at the dinner table. How many people will be eating dinner?"

Subtraction activities

Many everyday situations call for subtraction, but these activities focus on "take away" situations. When work-

ing with your child on subtraction, remember to use the terms *minus* and *equals* in addition to *take away* and *makes* or *leaves*. Encourage your child to verbalize what he or she is doing when working with objects.

- Place five beans on a paper plate. Ask your child to tell how many beans are on the plate. Then ask her or him to put one aside. Ask how many are left on the plate. Say, "Five beans minus one bean equals four beans." Repeat until no (zero) beans are left. Try this activity starting with ten beans.

- Make a subtraction problem using two different kinds of beans. Put five white beans on a paper plate and three red beans next to them. Ask your child to count the total number of beans, saying there are

eight beans. Have your child take away the five white beans, counting them as they are removed. Ask how many beans are left. Say, "Eight beans minus five beans equals three beans." Have your child push the beans back together, take away three red beans, and say the subtraction sentence, "Eight beans minus three beans equals five beans. "

- Write a subtraction problem on the erasable board. Ask your child to show the problem using buttons or macaroni. Encourage him or her to write the answer on the board.

- Have your child find and cut out a magazine picture of a group of things, for example, a group of people. Ask her or him to count the people and write the number on the erasable board. Cut two people from the picture and ask your child to write what you did (–2). Then have your child count the number of people left and write that number (= [?]). Continue this activity using the same picture until no people are left.

Extensions: Have your child give a subtraction problem while clearing the table after dinner. Start by counting the number of plates on the table. If four plates are started with and one is taken to the sink, three plates are are left on the table.

Measurement activities

When adults think of measurement, we think of rulers, measuring cups, bathroom scales, and so on. When young children first begin to measure, they deal with comparisons: heavier or lighter than, more or less than, bigger or smaller than. They do not need to use rulers or other standard units of measure, but they compare and measure with objects.

- Select any shoelace and mark it with some tape. Choose other shoelaces and ask your child to sort them by length. One group should be longer than the taped shoelace, one group shorter, and another may be about the same length. Ask your child to name the groups.

- Choose a group of macaroni pieces of approximately the same size. Lay out a piece of yarn. Ask your child to measure the yarn with the macaroni pieces by laying the macaroni end to end along the yarn. When finished, she or he should count the macaroni and say, "The yarn is six pieces of macaroni long."

- Use other objects, such as an unsharpened pencil, to measure items around the house. First find items that are longer than (taller), shorter than (smaller), or the same length as, the new pencil. Then measure the pencil length of various household items.

- Ask your child to break off clay pieces of different sizes and roll them into balls. Then have her or him group the balls on paper plates according to sizes: small balls, medium-sized balls, large (big) balls. Your child can also make clay "snakes" and order the lengths from shortest to longest.

- Push a chair up to the sink filled with water and allow your child to explore liquid measurement using various sizes of plastic cups, bowls, and other containers. Allow him or her to pour water from one container to another to discover which holds more, which holds less. This activity is also easy to do in the bathtub!

- Ask your child which is heavier—the bag of lima beans or the bag of yarn scraps. Have him or her hold one bag in each hand to check the prediction. Put a number of different types of canned goods and boxed foods on the table. Ask your child to make groups of items that are heavier than, lighter than, or the same as another item, for example, "These are heavier than the soup can; these are lighter."

Extensions: While grocery shopping, your child can make comparisons of the size and weight of items as they are added to the basket. Use terms of comparison, such as *more than* and *less than*, as well as *lighter than* and *bigger than.*

Conclusion

Parents can help their children's mathematical development by participating in a home-study program that complements the classroom curriculum. In this way, skills introduced at school are reinforced at home. By making available a scheduled, quiet time for children to do homework, parents are helping them develop good study habits as well as responsibility. By encouraging children to verbalize their thinking, parents are helping children develop problem-solving skills.

Schools, conversely, can help parents work with their children at home by offering assistance and encouragement in getting started. Parents have indicated that table-top mathematics

has become a popular evening activity. Many have expressed appreciation for the suggestions for simple learning activities. Some parents have been overheard discussing variations and extensions among themselves before and after school.

When schools assign relevant homework and give parents the tools needed to help their children, students have the advantage of extra practice in an informal, nongraded setting. Students, parents, and schools all benefit from a curriculum-related home-study program.

References

Bennett, William J. *First Lessons: A Report on Elementary Education in America.* Washington, D.C.: U.S. Department of Education, 1986.

Bristor, Valerie J. "But I'm Not a Teacher." *Academic Teacher* 23 (September 1987): 23–27.

Croft, Doreen J. *Parents and Teachers: A Resource Book for Home, School, and Community Relations.* Belmont, Calif.: Wadsworth Publishing Co., 1979.

Bibliography

Baratta-Lorton, Mary. *Mathematics Their Way.* Menlo Park, Calif.: Addison-Wesley Publishing Co., 1976.

Bruneau, Odette J. "Involving Parents in the Mathematics Education of Their Young Handicapped Child." *Arithmetic Teacher* 36 (December 1988): 16–18.

Flexer, Roberta J., and Carolyn L. Topping. "Mathematics on the Home Front." *Arithmetic Teacher* 36 (October 1988): 12–19.

Harcourt, Lalie. *Explorations for Early Childhood.* Toronto: Addison-Wesley Publishing Co., 1988.

Helping at Home

Kate Kline

Parents often ask for suggestions about activities to do with their young children at home to help further their mathematical understanding. Many of them have helped their children learn the counting sequence or recognize numerals, but they are also interested in activities that extend children's thinking about numbers and that the whole family can do together. Many school districts have adopted new Standards-based curricula that develop children's thinking in a way that may not be familiar to parents; therefore, they need assistance in doing at-home activities that are consistent with the development of number ideas in school.

Two types of activities help parents stimulate children's numerical thinking. One type involves highlighting everyday situations that require additive thinking, such as figuring out the number of treats needed for a birthday party or the number of utensils needed to set the table for a family of four. The

Kate Kline, kate.kline@wmich.edu, teaches in the department of mathematics and statistics at Western Michigan University, Kalamazoo, MI 49008. She taught for several years at the early-childhood level and currently works with preservice and in-service elementary school teachers. Readers are encouraged to send manuscripts for this section to the editor, Kate Kline, at the address above.

other type includes using group games. Games work well because the whole family can enjoy them and children love to play them over and over again, which allows them to practice a particular concept repeatedly. Kamii (1985, 121) discusses the value of games and why it is beneficial to encourage children to play games as an avenue to learning:

> While problems encountered in day-to-day life encourage logico-arithmetical reasoning, they do not lend themselves to repetitive acts of addition. It is in the context of play that children can practice addition. Group games provide an avenue for structured play, in which they are intrinsically motivated to think about and remember numerical combinations.

Group Games

It would be impossible to describe all the games that encourage children to develop number relationships. The following are a selection of the group games that I have found to be the most popular with children and parents. Some are variations of common games, such as go fish, whereas others are from new mathematics curricula. The games Racing Bears and On and Off are from the *Investigations in Number, Data, and Space* curriculum and Turn over 5 and 5s Go Fish are variations of games in that program. Cover Up was designed by the author.

Racing Bears

The object of the Racing Bears game is to capture counters from the tenth space on the game board (see fig. 1) by landing on the tenth space. See figure 2. To play the game, place counters on the tenth space on each track and place teddy bears on the start space on each track. Next, players or teams take turns rolling a die and moving any of the bears on the board the resulting number of spaces. Players or teams may use part of a roll to move a bear to the tenth space and then use the rest of the roll to move another bear on another track. For example, suppose that one bear is on the eighth space of its track and a player rolls a 3. The player may move

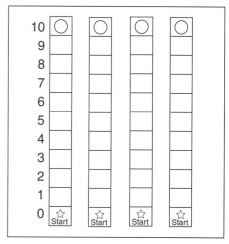

Fig. 1. The Racing Bears game board

Fig. 2. The Foerg family playing Racing Bears

the bear two spaces to the tenth space and then move a bear on another track one space. Once a tenth space is reached on a track, the player captures the counter, moves the teddy bear back to start, and places a new counter on the tenth space of that track.

As children play this game, ask them to explain how they figured out how many spaces to move and how they decided which bear to move. Observing how children break apart numbers when they move bears on two separate tracks yields information on how they think about number combinations. At first, they may not be able to figure out how to break apart a roll of 4 into two moves. Rather than tell them how, ask questions to prompt children's thinking to help them learn from the game. Have counters available, and after they show you four counters, ask, "Can you show me how you could make two separate piles with the four counters?" "Can you think of another way?" "Can we find a way to move two different teddy bears on the game board?" If children have difficulty splitting rolls, be patient. Over time, children will develop more sophisticated ways to think about numbers and the combinations that make up those numbers.

On and Off

The object of this activity is to toss counters over a piece of paper and record how many land on, and how many land off, the paper. This game can be played with a small group of children by giving each child a chance to make a toss and record his or her findings. To play the game, the player first decides how many counters to toss and writes this total number on the game grid shown. Next, the player lays a piece of paper on a flat surface, places the counters in a cup, and tosses them over the paper. He or she records on the game grid how many counters landed on, and how many landed off, the paper. The process is repeated five times until the game grid is filled.

Total number _____

On	Off

Once five rounds have been completed, ask children to look at the game grid and describe what they see. They should realize that the on-off

pairs are different ways to make the total number. A good question to ask is "Can you think of an on-off pair for the total number that is not listed on the game grid?" Children may also recognize that some numbers increase while others decrease. For example, one on-off pair may be 2 and 6 for 8, whereas another pair may be 3 and 5. The 2 increased by one and the 6 decreased by one. Many children will not recognize this pattern until they have played the game repeatedly. Ask children what they see on the game grid each time they play the game. With continual exposure to the game, they will learn to think more and more about patterns and numerical relationships.

Cover Up

The object of this game is to cover up two 10-frames completely using snap cubes. See figure 3. To prepare for the game, make a collection of trains with the snap cubes. Make eight trains of one color that are five cubes long and twenty trains of another color that are two cubes long. Also have available about forty single cubes of yet another color. The player rolls a die and takes that many cubes to cover the 10-frames on their game board. The player may take any combination of cubes to make the total rolled but is not allowed to pull apart any of the 2-trains or 5-trains. For example, a player who rolls a 6 may take one 5-train and one single cube or may take two 2-trains and two single cubes. Play continues until one player has completely covered up both 10-frames with snap cubes.

At first, allow children to fill up the 10-frames in any order. After playing the game for some time, introduce the following rules: (1) Fill up the 10-frames in order from left to right and (2) fill up the 10-frames from top to bottom. These rules make the game slightly more difficult because they limit the number of combinations per roll. For example, if a 6 was rolled, the player could not use three 2-trains

Fig. 3. The Venaleck family playing Cover Up

to cover up an empty 10-frame because he or she would place two 2-trains and then have to pull apart the last 2-train to finish covering the top row.

This game encourages children to think about counting in groups and combinations of groups. For example, when a child rolls a 6, it would be important to note whether she always counts out single cubes to place on the 10-frame or realizes that she can count out three groups of 2-trains or a 5-train and a single cube. You might also ask children to tell you how many cubes they have altogether on their two 10-frames at different times during the game. This information will let you know whether they are able to count in groups. At first, it should be expected that children will count all the cubes by ones, even though some are organized into 2-trains and 5-trains. This tactic does not mean that you should tell them to count by the number of existing groups. Again, the power of these games allows children to develop more-sophisticated strategies if the games are played repeatedly. When children have had the opportunity to think of strategies and develop them on their own, they will understand them better and use them more readily.

Turn over 5

The object of this Concentration-type game is to capture pairs of cards that add to 5. This game can be played with children in a small group in which each child is allowed one turn at a time or in which children play with a partner. See figure 4. Make a set of twenty-four numeral cards with four cards for each of the numbers 0 through 5. It is helpful to include pictures or objects on each card for children who may not yet recognize all these numerals. To play the game, mix up the cards and lay them facedown in four rows of six. Players take turns by choosing two cards to turn over, trying to find a combination that adds to 5. If they find one, they capture that pair. If they do not, they turn the cards back over for the next player. As they play, it is important to ask children how they know what two cards will add to 5. If they have one card turned over, ask them to explain to you what number they think they need to pair with that card.

This game helps solidify children's understand-

ing and recall of basic addition facts in an engaging way. It can easily be varied by using a different sum, such as 10, where children are encouraged to find pairs that add to those numbers. The game can also be played by adding to the deck four wild cards, which may be used to represent any numbers.

5s Go Fish

This game is a variation of the popular game of go fish. The same rules apply, but rather than search for pairs of the same number, a player searches for pairs of two numbers that add to 5 or to other numbers as appropriate. You can use the deck of cards that was created for the "turn over 5" game and include the wild cards for an added challenge. This game, too, allows children to practice their basic-fact knowledge while playing a stimulating and entertaining game.

Regardless of the types of games that you send home to parents, it is important to keep open the school-to-home lines of communication. A technique that works well is to include a response form along with directions for the games to encourage parents to

Fig. 4. The game of Turn over 5

write about their experiences. Information could be contained on a form for parents to fill out and submit after playing a specific game. You might ask parents to write their comments in a journal that could accompany game bags that students check out on a rotating basis. The advantage of including a journal with the games is that parents are then able to read comments by other parents who have played the games. Some questions that are particularly effective for stimulating discussion include, What did you think of this game? Did you like the game? Why or why not? What do you think your child learned from playing this game? What did you learn about your child while playing this game?

These questions also encourage parents to think about what children are able to learn from playing games and how powerful they are as teaching tools. One parent responded,

I never thought about changing the "go fish" game to have kids search for pairs that add to a specific number. What an easy way to change this game so that you can practice adding in a fun way. My kids loved this, and I figured out quickly which pairs they knew and did not know. And by changing the number to add to, we have been playing this over and over. I am amazed at how many new combinations they learn every time we play and am wondering now if we could use this same game to work on subtraction next year!

Problems from Everyday Situations

Parents can also be encouraged to take advantage of the many situations that occur in everyday life that require thinking about numbers. For example, ask children to figure out how many napkins must be placed on the table if you are inviting two neighbors to join the family for dinner. Also ask children to figure out how many years older they are than their younger sister or brother. This kind of comparison problem is challenging for young children because it does not involve an adding or subtracting action.

Another type of problem that provides an extra challenge for young children involves more than one solution. One example follows:

Suppose that you have eight Beanie Babies. Some of them are cats and some are dogs. How many of each could you have? How many cats? How many dogs?

This type of problem encourages children to explore numerical relationships, to think about different number combinations, and to begin to approach problems in a systematic fashion to find all possible solutions.

As children first begin to work on this type of problem, they will struggle with searching for more than one solution and with appropriate ways to represent their thinking on paper so that it is clear to others. Figures 5a and 5b show a range of solutions to a similar problem that involves trying to find how many peas and carrots can form a group of seven. Five-year-old Dan was able to think of only one possible combination for seven. Six-year-old Megan was able to find more than one combination and also indicated what each number represented. She realized that 3 and 4 could be considered twice if you think about the 4 as representing peas in one case and carrots in the other. You cannot tell from Dan's work if he was thinking about this dual representation of 3 and 4 even though he wrote them more than once.

Parents should be encouraged to ask their children these types of problems and expect that it will take time for children to clarify and refine their thinking. Schulman and Eston (1998) describe the value of revisiting this type of problem throughout the school year. They explain that even by the end of the year, only a few kindergarten students were able to find all combinations for a given problem. Even so, they learned that the students began to build important generalizations about numbers from working on these types of problems.

Conclusion

Sharing these ideas with parents will enhance the kind of help they offer their children. Some may question the value of playing games and view them as being frivolous. However, play is children's natural way to learn about their world. The engaging nature of games prompts children to play them repetitively, which allows them to practice important skills. In fact, one could argue that playing these games is even more beneficial than spending the same amount of time drilling basic facts using flash cards. Not only are the games more inspiring, but the potential for learning and reasoning about mathematics is much greater, as well.

Bibliography

Barta, James, and Diane Schaelling. "Games We Play: Connecting Mathematics and Culture in the Classroom." *Teaching Children Mathematics* 4 (March 1998): 388–93.

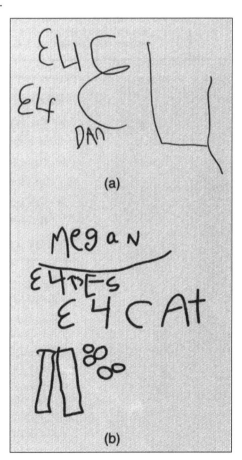

Fig. 5. Beginning representations of the solution to the peas-and-carrots problem

Caldwell, Marion Lee. "Parents, Board Games, and Mathematical Learning." *Teaching Children Mathematics* 4 (February 1998): 365–67.

Kamii, Constance. *Young Children Reinvent Arithmetic: Implications of Piaget's Theory.* New York: Teachers College Press, 1985.

Kamii, Constance, and R. DeVries. *Group Games in Early Education.* Washington, D.C.: National Association for the Education of Young Children, 1980.

Russell, Susan Jo, Cornelia Tierney, Jan Mokros, et al. *Investigations in Number, Data and Space.* Palo Alto, Calif: Dale Seymour Publications, 1998.

Schulman, Linda, and Rebeka Eston. "A Problem Worth Revisiting." *Teaching Children Mathematics* 5 (October 1998): 72–77.

Start Your Children's Mathematics-Literature Collection

Families may enjoy reading some children's books, such as those listed below, and using them to help create interesting activities or discussions around the home.

Axelrod, Amy. *Pigs on a Blanket.* New York: Simon & Schuster Children's Publishing Division, 1996. ISBN 0689-80505-5.

Hutchins, Pat. *The Doorbell Rang.* New York: Greenwillow Books, 1986. ISBN 0-688-09234-9.

Merriam, Eve. *12 Ways to Get to 11.* New York: Simon & Schuster Children's Publishing Division, 1993. ISBN 0671-75544-7.

Stevens, Janet. *Tops and Bottoms.* Orlando, Fla.: Harcourt Brace & Co., 1995. ISBN 0-15-292851-0.

Viorst, Judith. *Alexander, Who Used to Be Rich Last Sunday.* New York: Simon & Schuster Children's Publishing Division, 1978. ISBN 0689-71199-9.

Part 4
Appendixes

Appendix 1

Selected Readings and Activity Ideas from "Arithmetic Teacher" (AT) and "Teaching Children Mathematics" (TCM)

Baycliffe, Janie; Raymond Brie, and Beverly Oliver. "Teaching Mathematics with Technology: Family Math Enhanced through Technology." *AT* 41 (November 1993): 172–75.

Bruneau, Odette. "Involving Parents in the Education of Their Young Handicapped Child." *AT* 36 (December 1988): 16–18.

Franklin, Joyce, and Joyce Krebill. "Teacher to Teacher: Take-Home Kits." *AT* 40 (April 1993): 442–48.

Joseph, Helen. "Teaching Mathematics with Technology: Build Parental Support for Mathematics with Family Computers." *AT* 40 (March 1993): 412–15.

Lazerick, Beth. "News from the Net: Lesson Stop and Parents Guide to the Internet." *TCM* 5 (May 1999): 548.

Contains Web site reference: www.lessonstop.org

Lazerick, Beth and Judith Day Seidel. "Tech Times News from the Net: Helping Your Child Learn Math." *TCM* 3 (November 1996): 141.

Contains web site reference: www.ed.gov/pubs/parents/Math/

O'Connell, Susan R. "Math Pairs—Parents as Partners." *AT* 40 (September 1992): 10–12.

Peterson, Winnie. "Principles for Principals: Celebrate Math Month with a Family Math Night!" *AT* 36 (March 1989): 24–25.

Saarimaki, Peter. "Math by the Month: Celebrating Summer with Mathematics." *TCM* 3 (May 1997): 491–95.

Saarimaki, Peter, and Lorna Wiggan. "Math by the Month: Math in Your World." *TCM* 4 (May 1998): 521–25.

Szemcsak, Donna DeCasas, and Oliver J. West. "The Whole Town Is Talking about It ... 'Math Month,' That Is." *TCM* 3 (December 1996): 170–73.

Tregaskis, Owen. "Parents and Mathematical Games." *AT* 38 (March 1991): 14–16.

Young, Sharon. "Ideas." *AT* 38 (May 1991): 14–16.

Television-related data-collection activities

Appendix 2

Readings from "Teaching Children Mathematics: Focus Issue" (February 1998)

Anderson, Ann G. "Parents as Partners: Supporting Children's Mathematics Learning Prior to School," pp. 331–37.

Caldwell, Marion Lee. "Parents, Board Games, and Mathematical Learning," pp. 365–67.

Carey, Linda M. "Parents as Partners: A Successful Urban Story," pp. 314–19.

One teacher works with the parents of the children in her second-grade class

Coates, Grace Dávila, and Virginia Thompson. "Family Math by the Month," pp. 344–45.

Ehnebuske, Jean M. "In the Comfort of Their Own Homes: Engaging Families in Mathematics," pp. 338–43, 351.

Article discusses the successful implementation of the K–3 IMPACT project in Irving, Texas.

Ensign, Jacque. "Parents, Portfolios, and Personal Mathematics," pp. 346–51.

In an assessment activity, students work with their parents describing a home-based mathematical experience.

Ford, Marilyn Sue, Robin Follmer, and Kathleen K. Litz. "In Our Opinion: School-Family Partnerships: Parents, Children, and Teachers Benefit," pp. 310–12.

Hartog, Martin D., Maria Diamantis, and Patricia Brosnan. "Doing Mathematics with Your Child," pp. 326–30.

Article contains activity ideas and selected references.

Levine, Linda L. "Promising Research, Programs, and Projects: Networking to Make a Parent Project a Dream Come True," pp. 376–79.

Article describes a program in which parents are central to the planning, development, implementation, and evaluation. Program contents include leader's guide, parent's handbook, video segments, and a thirty-minute documentary.

McCarty, Diane. "Links to Literature: Books + Manipulatives + Families = A Mathematics Lending Library," pp. 368–75.

Article contains extensive references to children's literature.

Morse, Amy B., and Polly Wagner. "Learning to Listen: Lessons from a Mathematics Seminar for Parents," pp. 360–64, 375.

Peresinni, Dominic D. "What's All the Fuss about Involving Parents in Mathematics Education?", pp. 320–25.

Appendix 3

Selected Text Resources

Coates, Grace Dávila, and Jean Kerr Stenmark. *Family Math for Young Children: Comparing.* Berkeley, Calif.: Lawrence Hall of Science, University of California, Berkeley, 1997.

Cox, Jackie L., and Tom Lewis. *A Parent Handbook to Mathematics Grades K–6.* Park Forest, Ill.: Illinois Council of Teachers of Mathematics, n.d.

This handbook, available in multiples of 100 only, contains information for parents on helping with homework, statements regarding curricular changes and the role of technology, and lists of children literature books, selected Web sites, and other relevant resources. ICTM, P.O. Box 340, Park Forest, IL 60466-0340.

Hart, Amy, Mitzi Smyth, Kate Vetter, and Eric Hart. "Children, Teach Your Parents Well: Communication in Mathematics between Home and School." In *Communication in Mathematics, K–12 and Beyond,* 1996 Yearbook of the National Council of Teachers of Mathematics, edited by Portia Elliott, pp. 180–86. Reston, Va.: National Council of Teachers of Mathematics, 1996.

Hynes, Michael C. *Ideas: NCTM Standards-Based Instruction, Grades 1–4.* Reston, Va.: National Council of Teachers of Mathematics, 1995.

This collection of "Ideas" from *AT* and *TCM* contains eight family activities complete with blackline masters, activity objectives, directions, and possible extensions (pp. 104–19).

———. *Ideas: NCTM Standards-Based Instru Grades 5–8.* Reston, Va.: National Council of Teach Mathematics, 1996.

This collection of "Ideas" from *AT* and *TCM* contains n family activities complete with blackline masters, activ objectives, directions, and possible extensions (pages 110–29).

Kanter, Patsy, and Cynthia Hearn Dorfman, eds. *H Your Child Learn Math with Activities for Ch Aged 5 through 13.* Washington, D.C.: Office of I tional Research and Improvement, U.S. Departm Education, 1992. ED 355122.

Leeson, Neville. *Helping Your Child with Mathema Parents' Guide.* Bruwood, Victoria, Australia: Del 1997.

Stenmark, Jean Kerr, Virginia Thompson, and Ruth C *Family Math.* Berkeley, Calif.: Lawrence Hall of Sc University of California at Berkeley, 1986.

Contains information on organizing Family Math nights including lesson-plan ideas, blackline masters and direc and an extensive list of resources for parents.

Thompson, Virginia, and Karen Mayfield-Ingram. *F Math—the Middle School Years: Algebraic Reas and Number Sense.* Berkeley, Calif.: Lawrence F Science, University of California at Berkeley, 1998.

The focus of this resource, as the title implies, relates t organizing Family Math events for middle school studei and their parents. Other sections include additional hel resources and information parent-advocacy issues.